Advance Pr

"For those Rome visitors, w

sighting for more sites to co.., ..., ...us unu Jilvia Prosperi have good
news for you! Their guidebook, *103 Other Adventures In and Around Rome*,
opens a great new vista for fun and exploration with the family. For Bill Richards'
third effort in his travel series geared to families with kids, he teamed up with
Roman tour guide Silvia Prosperi to delve into the wealth of things to see and
do in Rome and its region of Lazio. Teaching as it inspires, *103 Other Adventures
In and Around Rome* starts with a chronological organization of sites. This
provides a helpful introduction to the millennia of history from Etruscans to
Romans to Popes to Revolutionaries. The book then unfolds into what might be
described as a three-star menu of activities arranged by individual tastes. Want
art? Choose from Classic to Contemporary. Walks, wine, water sports, and more,
a complete feast right down to a sweet treat in Rome's century-old chocolate
shop! This book is a terrific resource for locals as well as tourists, as Prosperi
and Richards have found about every treasure Lazio has to offer (who knew
there was the world's fastest zipline twenty-five miles south of Rome?).

   Furthermore, this is a guidebook that is not only a wealth of material but
is user friendly. *103 Other Adventures In and Around Rome* breaks down each
site by the most common questions any parent (or tourist) would ask: what is
it, how much does it cost, how do I get there, and, the all-important, is it worth
it? The collaboration of tour guide and parent not only makes each site feel
like a must-see but renders the voyage feasible. They strike a perfect balance
between understanding what tots, teens, and tweens will enjoy and how to
get the most out of the travel experience.

   After all the impediments of travel during the pandemic, *103 Other
Adventures In and Around Rome* will inspire (and help!) parents to pack up
the kids and move beyond the crowded tourist magnets to plumb the depths
of Lazio (did I mention the caves?). Most importantly, the fine work of these
authors will remind readers, after a year of living virtually, how rewarding the
real experiences of seeing, climbing, swimming, tasting, and yes, ziplining are."

Elizabeth Lev
Tour Guide, Art Historian, and Author

"Rome has a way of getting under your skin; the more of it you see, the more of it you want to discover. Having lived in Rome for over nine years, I quickly learnt that some of the most exciting parts of the city are not found in typical guidebooks. This book is different. It takes you out of "touristy" Rome and introduces you to adventures that help you to fill historical knowledge gaps and see the city in a deeper way. It's full of ideas for repeated visits. After reading this book, you will be quickly planning your next trip to Rome to explore the next chapter."

Karen Ryder
Emeritus Exploring Rome Group Coordinator

103 Other Adventures In and Around Rome*

*Beyond the biggies like the Colosseum, the Pantheon, and the Vatican

By Bill Richards & Silvia Prosperi

RUMBLE
BOOKS

PRESENTED BY *A FRIEND IN ROME & FAMILY ON THE LOOSE*

FRONT COVER PHOTOGRAPHY
TOP (L–R) Sky Experience; Adobe Stock; Luca Pietrosanti
BOTTOM (L–R): Adobe Stock; Miceli Vela; Enrico Fontolan

INTERIOR PHOTOGRAPHY
Patrizio Fortuna: page 298

Silvia Prosperi: pages iv, 3, 18, 32, 39, 45, 56, 91, 105, 117, 123, 134, 141, 144, 150, 162, 224, 229, 230, 251,269, 274, 288

Bill Richards: pages 10, 27, 109, 115, 125, 147, 182, 205, 207, 218, 236, 247, 248, 260, 266, 272, 277, 298

Adobe Stock: pages 6, 9, 14, 21, 23, 29, 35, 42, 47, 54, 59, 64, 66, 68, 70, 73, 75, 82, 84, 88, 94, 96, 99, 100, 103, 111, 120, 153, 156, 158, 161, 171, 175, 179, 190, 195, 198, 210, 221, 253, 29

ILLUSTRATIONS
© Patrizio Fortuna: pages xii, 2, 16, 49, 80, 107, 130,132, 154, 173, 186, 188, 203, 217, 226, 242, 258, 279, 286

Adobe Stock: page 244

MAPS
Zoey Richards: page 297

First Edition: November 2021
Library of Congress Control Number (LCCN): 2021916998
ISBN: 978-0-9886356-1-6

Published by Rumble Books
info@rumblebooks.com

Acknowledgements

We have so many people to thank for helping us produce this book. First and foremost, we thank our families who supported and partnered with us in our travel and life adventures.

Bill would like to thank his parents, Bill and Fearn Richards, for first showing him that the world is a wonderful place to explore. His wife, Ashley Steel, encouraged us at every hesitation and provided invaluable suggestions throughout the writing and publishing process. His daughters also provided important support, with Zoey Richards making the maps for the book and Logan Richards acting as the director of digital outreach for *Family on the Loose*.

Silvia would like to thank her family for their support in every new project she has undertaken, particularly her son Mattia for being so patient during the long video calls with Bill during the writing of this book! A special thanks to Antonio for walking many miles during the last three years in every kind of weather, consuming all of his annual leave days to explore hidden corners of Lazio. Silvia's friends and colleagues have enhanced her inherent curiosity and have always been ready to try new adventures together.

And we'd both like to thank the Explore Rome Group, which is where we met and this fun book writing adventure began.

Many tour guides associated with *A Friend in Rome* and *Around Rome Day Trips*, who we are happy to call friends, were very kind to double check our initial drafts in their area of expertise: Nicole Ciceroni, Irene Chinappi, Federica Dal Palù, Francesca Di Marzo, Arianna Fusco, Irene Maestri, Laura Nicotra, Micaela Pavoncello, Luca Pietrosanti, Elena Ronca, and Daniela Stampatori. Patrizio Fortuna created illustrations specifically for the book. Amanda Elkin edited the text and vastly improved our writing. Matt Mayerchak and Laura Glassman are the awesome graphic design team that made the book so beautiful.

Roman Numeral Primer: It seemed logical to have the adventures in this book identified by Roman numerals. Here's a key to how the system works:

I = 1	VI = 6	XI = 11	XVI = 16	XX = 20	LX = 60	C = 100
II = 2	VII = 7	XII = 12	XVII = 17	XXX = 30	LXX = 70	CI = 101
III = 3	VIII = 8	XIII = 13	XVIII = 18	XL = 40	LXXX = 80	CII = 102
IV = 4	IX = 9	XIV = 14	XIX = 19	L = 50	XC = 90	CIII = 103
V = 5	X =10	XV = 15				

Contents

Chapter 4: The Renaissance (15th to 17th centuries)

Chapter 5: Enlightenment, Unification, and Mussolini

Chapter 6: Classics

Chapter 7: Modern

Chapter 8: Music

Chapter 9: Hill Towns

Chapter 10: Food & Wine

Chapter 11: Walking & Hiking

Chapter 12: Thrills

Chapter 13: The Sea Beaches

Chapter 14: The Lakes

Chapter 15: The Rivers

Chapter 16: The Pools

Introduction

Rome is truly an amazing place, but you don't need this book to tell you that. There is literally history around every corner. The food is fresh and fantastic, the culture is storied and vibrant, and the people have a zest for life that is infectious.

This "guide" book is for people that have been to Rome before or are spending an extended period of time in the Eternal City. It does not include the biggest named places that you likely came to Rome the first time to see: the Colosseum, the Forum, the Pantheon, Trevi Fountain, or the Vatican. Instead, it highlights the myriad of other places of interest and adventure: places that help fill gaps in the historical story of ancient Rome; places that illuminate the past and present of Rome's art and music culture; places like hilltop villages and swimming holes that provide an escape from the city's busyness within a short train ride.

This book is for people who want to "level-up" in their Rome discoveries. It is for people looking for adventures beyond the tourist core. It is for families. It is for day-trippers. It is for history nerds looking for a deeper understanding. It is for people comfortable with public transportation and also for people who prefer driving a car. It is for people who are both adventurous and curious about the world around them.

With a few exceptions, most of the adventures in this book are in the region of Lazio, which is where the city of Rome is located. Lazio is made up of five provinces: Rome in the middle, Viterbo and Rieti to the north, and Frosinone and Latina to the south. Each of the adventures can be accomplished in a day or less, though the ones at the edges of Lazio might be better explored on a weekend when you have more time.

This book does not attempt to detail all the information you might want to know about a place. Rather, it identifies and describes the sights and adventures you should not miss during your extended explorations of Rome. The rest is up to you — we don't want to compromise your sense of self-discovery when you get to these places.

The adventures in this book follow a similar format. First, we offer a short description of the adventure and why you might want to go there. Next, we discuss where it is and how to get there. This section includes public transit options, but many adventures are off the beaten path and require your own transportation, be that a taxi, a car share, a rental, or your own little Fiat (tips for driving in Rome is a whole different book!). Scooter and bicycle rentals are also readily available to access adventures within the city. All distances given in this section are "as the crow flies" from *Piazza Venezia* in *Centro Storico* (the central neighborhood of Rome). There is also an estimate of the time and money needed for each adventure, though these variables depend on your haste and desired comfort. Please note that much of this book was written during the COVID-19 pandemic lockdowns. Some site details, such as entrance fees or opening times, were modified during this time to adhere to travel restrictions and are subject to change when normal operations resume. Please also note that we only include adult pricing, since entry fees for children or students typically vary on a sliding scale. Everything **FREE** is noted as such.

For families, we estimate the age suitability for each adventure, from toddlers to teens, and we recommend whether hiring a guide would enhance your adventure. Generally, if the adventure has anything to do with the history of Rome, having a guide that brings stories to life and fills your imagination with the subtleties of the time is utterly invaluable.

And finally, we recommend the best time to go on each adventure, offer fun facts, and suggest activities to enrich your experience. We have also included websites for each adventure, but encourage you to exercise your own skill at searching for the additional information you might need before heading out. Many of the websites are in Italian, but look to use the "translate" feature through your browser or a link to an English version of the site.

We wrote this book to share our love of Rome and illustrate the diversity of exploration possible in the entire region of Lazio, which has over 2,500 years of history. Bill is a travel writer who has lived in and visited many places in the world, including as a family with his wife and two kids. Silvia is a professional tour guide who knows more about Rome than just about anyone. Together, we make an inquisitive and experienced team who are always looking for the next adventure.

PART ONE

Historical
Adventures

The Etruscan Period

Vulci

Vulci was an Etruscan city that predated the founding of Rome by some 150 years. Dating back to at least the 9th century BC, Vulci was one of the primary centers of Etruscan society, which was generally organized into an association of city-states. From its peak around 750 BC, Etruscan culture conflicted with Rome until Etruscan cities were formally absorbed into Rome in 280 BC. Today, Vulci is a 120-hectare archeological park with fascinating ruins surrounded by farmers' fields near the present-day border of Lazio and Tuscany. There are fine examples of the houses of the wealthy, a polytheistic temple, and an ancient Roman road. There are also walking trails along the beautiful Fiora River, a visitor center, and a couple of nearby restaurants. Just upstream of the park is a 12th-century castle (*Castello dell'Abbadia*) that houses the National Museum of Vulci and is adjacent to the beautiful *Ponte dell'Abbadia*, a bridge that dates to the 1st century and still spans the river.

Why go? Ultimately, this is a walk in a country landscape that has been modified very little over the last 2,000 years. First, you can learn about the history of the Etruscans by exploring the ruins of Vulci and the museum. Then, you can enjoy a stroll along the river, passing by rare long-horned Maremmana cattle and taking in the beautiful views of the ancient bridge.

 Where? Vulci is 92 kilometers northwest of Rome and it takes roughly an hour and 45 minutes to drive there by car.

 Cost and time? The archeological park costs €10/person, or €20 for a family ticket. The museum in the castle is only €4/person. To see both the park and the museum will take at least half a day.

 Kids? There's a decent amount of walking to get around the whole park, but it's possible to only do what you're comfortable with. At the least, a walk down to *Lago del Pellicone*, a large pool in the river, is worthwhile and the castle has a classic water-filled moat that is uniquely beautiful.

 Guide? A guide will be able to bring this quiet place to life. Either arrange ahead of time with your favorite Rome guide, consult a local guide (*Percorsi Etruschi*), or ask at the visitor center.

 When? Good weather days. It's very warm in the summer, but you can stick your feet in the river to cool off!

FUN FACTS

* Many movies have been filmed at Vulci including *Ladyhawke* (1985) and *Tale of Tales* (2015).
* Maremmana is a breed of cattle that has been on the Italian peninsula for thousands of years. They are typically light brown to grey and have large horns. While they were once used as draught animals, they are now primarily raised for their meat. They are adapted to poor pasture lands and can live semi-wild in challenging terrain.

Enrichment: *There are agriturismi (independently owned farmstays, see Adventure #CIII) with thermal pools near Vulci if you'd like to make a weekend of it. Combine with visits to Cerveteri, Tarquinia, or Santa Severa (other Etruscan-themed adventures in this book) for an excellent immersive Etruscan weekend. Round out the Etruscan experience with a visit to the National Etruscan Museum in* Villa Giulia *in Rome.*

www.vulci.it

www.polomusealelazio.beniculturali.it/index.php?it/551/museo
-archeologico-di-vulci

www.percorsietruschi.it

The Etruscan Necropolis at Cerveteri

This necropolis, a UNESCO World Heritage Site, is essentially a large Etruscan cemetery outside the town of Cerveteri. Dating from the 9th to 3rd centuries BC, there are roughly 1,000 tombs over 400 hectares, of which 10 hectares are enclosed in an outdoor museum. Etruscan families were typically entombed communally along with pottery and jewelry. Some tombs are impressively large circular mounds (called tumulus) with several entry points for different branches of the same family, while others are built in long rows along pathways. Examples of the items found in the tombs can be seen at the museum in town and at the National Etruscan Museum at *Villa Giulia* in Rome.

Why go? The information that can be gleaned about an ancient society from how they treated their dead is amazing. The physical structures of the tombs are remarkable, and getting lost amongst the curvy paths and

endless doorways beckoning you inside is easy. Entrance to the outdoor archeological park, which is a great place to simply walk, includes an interesting audio tour through a subset of the tombs, which takes you into the dark (but not in a scary way). The artifacts in the museum are also worth seeing.

 Where? The necropolis is 34 kilometers west-northwest from Rome and it takes over an hour to drive there. There is also a train to Ladispoli where you can transfer to a bus to Cerveteri. The archeological park is less than 2 kilometers outside of town.

Cost and time? The entrance to either the necropolis or the museum is €8/person. But if you go to both it is only €10. Together they will take about half a day. It's less than a five-minute drive between the necropolis and the museum.

 Kids? Despite the basically somber subject matter, or maybe because of it, the necropolis is a fascinating place. It's probably too much for young kids but teens will likely be interested, particularly in "getting lost" within the maze of ancient tombs.

 Guide? Yes! There are many more stories to be told than can be included on the audio tour. It might be possible to arrange to meet a licensed guide at the necropolis.

 When? Since the most interesting part of the adventure is out-side, it's better to go when the weather is good. Avoid the heat of the day in the summer.

FUN FACTS

* Etruscan tombs can resemble homes, with rooms, carved beds, and vaulted ceilings.
* As of 2021, there are 1,121 UNESCO World Heritage Sites in 167 countries, including 55 in Italy. Fifty of Italy's sites are "Cultural" like Cerveteri, and five are "Natural" like the Ancient Beech Forests in the Abruzzo region.

Enrichment: *The beach at Ladispoli is not far away and can be combined with Cerveteri to make a full-day trip. Other Etruscan adventures nearby to Cerveteri include Vulci, Tarquinia, and Santa Severa.*

≡ www.comune.cerveteri.rm.it/turismo-e-cultura/le-necropoli/la-banditaccia

The Etruscan Necropolis at Tarquinia

The Necropolis of Monterozzi is part of the same UNESCO World Heritage listing as the Necropolis of Cerveteri, with both dating back to the Etruscans of the 9th century BC. Outside the town of Tarquinia, this necropolis has over 6,000 tombs including impressive tumulus circular mounds. The primary difference between the Necropolis of Monterozzi and the Necropolis of Cerveteri is the many painted frescoes that have survived inside the tombs at Monterozzi, depicting life and landscapes from 2,500 years ago. The frescoes are an essential part of the first chapter of Italian art history. Some of the paintings have been moved into town at the National Etruscan Museum of Tarquinia.

Why go? Visiting both Tarquinia and Cerveteri completes the image of an Etruscan necropolis. All the tombs at Tarquinia are underground and more spread out than the tombs of Cerveteri, which are tightly packed, making it easy to get lost. Tarquinia's paintings also extend the understanding of early Italian life during the Etruscan civilization.

 Where? Tarquinia is 71 kilometers west-northwest of Rome and it takes about an hour and half to drive there. There is also a train from Rome to Civitavecchia, with a connecting bus to Tarquinia.

 Cost and time? The entrance fee for the necropolis is €6/adult, or €10 including entrance into the museum in town. The outdoor area at Monterozzi is relatively small compared to Cerveteri, and to see both the tombs and museum at Tarquinia will take at least half the day. The museum and the tombs are about a kilometer apart. A ticket for the museums and necropolis in both Tarquinia and Cerveteri is €15/adult.

 Kids? The somber subject matter may make it a challenge for younger kids. Cerveteri may be more fun for the "hide-and-go-seek" aspect of the tomb layout.

 Guide? Absolutely. Getting an educated interpretation of the paintings in the museum will create a more accurate image of Etruscan life. Afterward, you can explore Monterozzi on your own.

 When? Like many outdoor venues, the heat of the day in the summer is a challenge. In this case, all the tombs are under-ground, which is inherently cooler. Please note, the site is closed on Mondays.

FUN FACTS

* Necropolis means "city of the dead".
* The Italian town of Corneto was renamed in 1922 to the ancient name of Tarquinia, as the archeological exploration of the ancient site gained momentum.

Enrichment: *Visit other Etruscan sites, like Marturanum and* Villa Giulia *for the full dose of Etruscan history. There are also interesting ruins at* Ara della Regina *(outside of Tarquinia) and* Castel d'Asso *(outside of Viterbo), which are FREE.*

www.polomusealelazio.beniculturali.it/index.php?it/556/museo
-archeologico-nazionale-di-tarquinia

www.civitavecchia.portmobility.it/en/tarquinia-and-etruscan-necropolis
-monterozzi

ADVENTURE #IV

Marturanum

At its peak around the 6th century BC, Marturanum was an Etruscan village in what is now northern Lazio. As Etruscan society declined and the Roman Republic came to dominate the region, the people of Marturanum moved and consolidated into the present-day village of Barbarano Romano. Today, there isn't much left of the original Marturanum except for some walls and

the ruins of a few houses and temples. But there are extensive Etruscan tombs carved into the nearby rock faces in a beautiful stream gorge. The area is protected by a 1,240-hectare Regional Natural Park, which has an extensive trail system that links the archeological sites together through the forests, meadows, and gorge overlooks.

Why go? Go to Marturanum to remember that, over 2,500 years ago and long before the Romans came to rule the region, there was a thriving Etruscan society in Italy with their own language and culture. From the parking area there is a trail that heads steeply down into a forested stream gully where coming upon the tomb openings in the rock walls feels like discovering the ruins for the first time. Most of the tombs are underground, cave-like excavations, with roof reliefs and "beds" for the dead, but there are also a couple of round tumuli. On the other side of the creek are the ruins of the village itself. Just a short walk farther from the ruins of Marturanum is a small 12th-century church where monks lived until the 19th century, named after *San Giuliano* (Saint Julian the Hospitaller). Near the church is *Bagno Romano*, an "underground" bath perched inside the wall of a gorge that has beautiful landscape views.

Marturanum is an excellent excuse to get outside for a walk in the woods (bring your dog if you have one!). The trails to the ruins are very well marked and maintained, though there are some steep parts. There is also a small park museum in Barbarano Romano.

 Where? Barbarano Romano is 52 kilometers northwest of central Rome, and it takes about 75 minutes to drive there. It is also possible to inefficiently get there by train, but the closest station at Capranica-Sutri is still a 15-minute taxi ride. The parking area for the archeological part of the park is a couple of kilometers northeast of town.

 Cost and time? Walking in the nature park is FREE. It will take several hours to wander around the ruins and tombs. There is a picnic area at the car park, which also has a small shop that sells drinks and mementos.

 Kids? Yes. It is basically an outdoor walk in the woods with a big dose of Etruscan history thrown in. You can also visit Marturanum on horseback with the group Antiquitates. They also do archeology labs for kids. Keep an eye on the kids when the trail gets steep.

 Guide? There are frequent signs describing what you are seeing, but an expert guide will help fill in the stories of the place. If you choose to come by horse, the trail ride will include a guide with knowledge of Marturanum.

 When? Anytime, really. The cold water in the stream keeps the gully quite cool.

FUN FACTS

* The icon for the nature park is a deer nose-to-nose with a dog, which is carved into a wall above one of the ancient stairways leading down to one of the tombs.
* Over some of the tomb entrances, rectangular banquet rooms can be seen where the Etruscan celebrated their ancestors.
* Saint Julian is known for building homes and hospitals for the poor as penance for mistakenly killing his own parents, erroneously thinking they were his wife and her lover.

Enrichment: *The medieval walled town of Barbarano Romano is beautiful and worth a wander after visiting Marturanum.* Lago di Vico *is only 10 kilometers northeast of Barbarano Romano.*

www.parchilazio.it/marturanum
www.antiquitates.it

Villa Giulia

Villa Giulia is a palace built in the mid-16th century by Pope Julius III. At the time, it sat at the edge of Rome and had access to the Tiber River. The back of the villa has a semi-circular courtyard that leads to a *nympheum*, a sunken garden where the shade and fountains provide a refreshing summer environment. After the death of the pope, the ownership of the villa was assumed by the Church, and then confiscated by the Italian government in 1870. Today, the villa sits at the northern edge of *Villa Borghese* and is home to the National Etruscan Museum (*Museo Nazionale Etrusco*).

Why go? Like many villas turned into museums, there is both the beauty of the palace as well as the history of the archeological exhibits. In this case, the beauty is seeing the frescoes along the villa courtyard and the sunken nympheum while learning about Etruscan society, which predates the ancient Romans. There are over 6,000 objects in the 50 rooms of the museum, many found in the necropoli at Cerveteri, Veio, and Vulci.

 Where? *Villa Giulia* is about 2.5 kilometers north of *Piazza Venezia*. The 19 tram passes by the front of the museum, as well as the National Gallery of Modern and Contemporary Art just up the street. The closest subway stop is Flaminio on the A Line, but it is still 750 meters and a 15-minute walk away.

 Cost and time? The entrance fee to get into *Villa Giulia* is €10/person. Seeing the museum will take a couple of hours.

 Kids? Maybe, but the artifacts start to get a little redundant after a while, even for the adult layperson. The museum is worth it, though, to learn about what was out there before Rome existed. Ask your Rome guide for a kid-friendly tour.

 Guide? Absolutely! But if you can't find an in-person guide, in the bookstore of the museum you can rent an audio guide (€5) and they also have short written guides, including one for kids, to provide information about what you are seeing.

 When? A bad weather day! The museum is typically closed on Mondays.

FUN FACTS

✳ The Etruscans were skilled sailors and were known throughout the Mediterranean, sometimes as pirates. Much of what we know about them today is from their necropoli because their villages were largely destroyed from centuries of conflict with the Romans.

✳ A nympheum is a shrine dedicated to nymphs and is usually associated with water. The source of the water for the nympheum in *Villa Giulia* is the *Acqua Vergine* aqueduct, the same as for the Trevi Fountain.

✳ Much of the villa was never completed after the death of Pope Julius III, but there are three rooms upstairs that still have their original frescoes.

Enrichment: Villa Poniatowski, *a smaller residence just down the street from* Villa Giulia, *is also part of the museum and is included in the entrance fee. It is usually open from April to October, but not every day. Also just up the street from* Villa Giulia, *but in the other direction, is the National Gallery of Modern and Contemporary Art as well as everything that* Villa Borghese *has to offer. And don't forget about the other Etruscan adventures in this book. The exhibits of* Villa Giulia *will be more exciting after you've visited the places where the artifacts were found.*

☰ www.museoetru.it/en

Ancient Rome

The Appian Way

At one point during the Roman Empire the adage "All roads lead to Rome" was certainly true. The Appian Way (*Via Appia Antica*) is the first of the many paved ancient Roman roads. The road heads southeast from the city toward Capua (north of Naples) and on to the Adriatic coast at Brindisi, covering a total distance of 563 kilometers. Initiated in 312 BC to move troops for placating what is now the Campania countryside, it was completed in 264 BC (though modifications continued for centuries). Today, the beginning of the road is part of a 4,580-hectare park system (*Parco Regionale dell'Appia Antica*) that protects many ancient historic sites over the first 11 miles or so (the distances on the Appian Way are typically listed in miles rather than kilometers).

The Appian Way begins at *Circus Maximus* and passes through the Aurelian Wall at the Appia Gate (*Porta San Sebastiano*), also the site of the Museum of the Walls (*Museo delle Mura*). The ancient sites, including villas, another circus, and many catacombs and mausoleums, are identified by mileage along the road. Unfortunately, the first couple of miles outside the gate are not very pedestrian-friendly, as walls have been constructed to the exclusion of sidewalks. But farther along, the walls end and the traffic is less terrorizing. Indeed, on Sundays the road is typically closed to traffic and is a great place for a walk or a bicycle ride. Currently, the road is made mostly of cobblestones with short sections of the original ancient paving stones before becoming more of a dirt track for the last few miles.

Why go? There are so many reasons: enjoying a nice day outside, bicycling, visiting the Catacombs of Callixtus, San Sebastian Basilica, Circus of Maxentius, Cecilia Metella's Mausoleum, *Capo di Bove*, Quintili's Villa. And that's not even half of the sites in the first few miles. You can easily cycle

the first 16 kilometers of the road with ancient sites all along the way, and
then turn around and come back. Or you can just walk as far as you want.

 Where? The 118 bus heads out from *Circus Maximus* southeast
along *Viale delle Terme di Caracalla*, which turns into *Via di Porta
San Sebastiano*, which turns in to *Via Appia Antica*. It's really just
a straight shot. The bus goes along the Appian Way until just after
the San Sebastian Basilica, when it turns left. At the very latest,

get off at the church. That's where the traffic thins out and is a good place to start walking/biking.

 Cost and time? Walking along the Appian Way is FREE. There are several places to rent bicycles along the road, starting at about €16 for a half day (shorter times are available too). Some of the sites have entrance fees, but many of them are FREE. There are enough things to see along the road, and it is long enough that you can easily spend a whole day exploring.

 Kids? Yes. The littlest kids might be not able to walk far and the cobblestones are not terribly stroller friendly, but there is so much history to see along the Appian Way. It is especially enjoyable on the car-free days. The parks along the way are perfect for picnics!

 Guide? Yes! As with most ancient historical sites, the Appian Way is better explored with someone who knows the stories of the place. This is especially true for the first few miles of the road, where the sites are relatively close together.

 When? Sundays when the weather is nice and the traffic is controlled. But every day after about mile 4 the traffic naturally thins because the road is generally too bumpy for most drivers.

~~~~~~

FUN FACTS

* During the height of its busiest period in history, the road was lined with grand mausoleums in homage to the wealthy families of Rome. Much of the material used to build these elaborate cemeteries was later pilfered to build other things.

* Following their revolt led by Spartacus, 6,000 enslaved people were crucified along the Appian Way outside of Capua in 71 BC.

~~~~~~

ADVENTURE #VII

Ostia Antica

Ostia Antica was the port city that once served as the seaward gateway to ancient Rome. Active for over 1,000 years from at least the 4th century BC, Ostia, as it was known then, reached its peak population of about 50,000 people in the 3rd century AD before declining with the fortunes of ancient Rome until it was finally abandoned in the 6th century. Once located at the mouth of the Tiber River (*ostia* is a Latin derivation of "mouth"), the site is now more than 4 kilometers from where the river flows into the sea due to new land created by the deposition of river sediment.

The Archeological Park of Ostia Antica is 55 hectares and encompasses extensive ruins of the ancient city, including residences, temples, and warehouses. There is the Square of Guilds, where kiosks around a courtyard housed various sea trading associations as depicted by the elaborate mosaics on each kiosk floor. There is also a large theater that is occasionally still active today, and one of the oldest synagogues in Europe. You can see a public latrine and a fullery, where human urine was used to clean

and dye clothes. And you can visit what may be the best-known features of Ostia Antica: the extensive mosaics on the floors of the public baths.

Why go? Most of the ancient city of Ostia Antica is included in the archeological park. Centered on the main east-west classic Roman stone street, *Decumanus Maximus*, the city's sites stretch for over a kilometer. Wandering down the alleys and exploring the open doorways is fun and exciting, and there are unique things to learn around every corner. There is a museum, a café, and a bookstore on site. Ostia Antica is often compared to Pompeii but is much easier to reach from Rome.

 Where? Ostia Antica is 22 kilometers southwest from central Rome. It has a designated train station on the line from Rome-Ostiense to the modern town of Ostia. It's roughly a 500-meter walk from the station to the park entrance.

 Cost and time? The entrance fee to the Archeological Park of Ostia Antica is €12/person. The ruins are extensive and the park is

really too big to see in one visit, so there is an annual pass
available for €25.

 Kids? There's a decent amount of walking and the site is not
stroller-friendly, so little kids will wear out way before you've been
able to see much. But imagining the life that teemed through
these streets 2,000 years ago will intrigue most teens and tweens.

 Guide? Yes! There is an extensive audio guide for rent at the
entrance of the park. Although there is a lot of good information in
the audio guide, it is long and not terribly entertaining.

 When? The park is outside, so go on a good weather day
and avoid the heat of a summer afternoon. The site is closed
on Mondays.

~~~~~~

FUN FACTS

* In the Middle Ages and the Renaissance, building materials were
salvaged from the abandoned Ostia Antica to help build churches and
villas as far away as Pisa and Amalfi.

* Archeological excavation of the ruins began in the 19th century but
accelerated under Mussolini.

~~~~~~

Enrichment: *Combine your adventure at Ostia Antica with Portus (see
the next adventure) and the newly renovated Museum of Roman Ships
at Fiumicino.*

www.ostiaantica.beniculturali.it/en/home/

www.ostia-antica.org

www.sovraintendenzaroma.it/i_luoghi/roma_antica/monumenti/monte
_testaccio

Portus

Ancient Rome needed a more dependable seaport to supply the growing city with resources from afar, so the Emperors Claudius and Trajan built one north of Ostia Antica in the 1st and 2nd centuries AD. It included a 39-hectare hexagonal cement-lined basin that was eight meters deep and large enough to fit 200 ships at one time. Goods were transferred at the port from seafaring ships to warehouses and then onto riverboats for the last leg of the journey up the Tiber River to Rome. Portus was active for more than 500 years. The basin is now a conservation area for wildlife, and archeologists are still exploring the ruins of the ancient warehouses. It is also now more than 3 kilometers from the coast, as the sea retreated from accumulated deposition.

Why go? Portus is an important part of the story of ancient Rome. It succeeded Ostia Antica as Rome's primary port and was vital to the standard of living of Rome's population. After 1,900 years, the port basin, now called *Lago di Traiano*, is still intact and many of the town's warehouses are still standing. It is a beautiful place to walk. The *Oasi di Porto*, which includes *Lago di Traiano*, is a private park owned by the Barberini family that is primarily managed as an ecological reserve.

 Where? Portus is adjacent and south of Fiumicino Airport, which is about 23 kilometers southwest of Centro. A car would be useful to get there, though you can catch a local train or the Leonardo Express from Rome to the airport and then take a short taxi ride from the terminal.

 Cost and time? The Imperial Harbours of Claudius and Trajan Park, which has ruins of warehouses and views of the basin, are FREE. It is open only a couple of days per week, so check on the website before you go. You can cover the site in a couple of hours, though on a nice day it would also be a good place for a picnic. The *Oasi di Porto*, which is periodically open to the public, costs €12/adult.

 Kids? All ages will enjoy both parks although there is walking involved. Like other places in Rome, strollers can be a challenge.

 Guide? The parks are a pleasant walk on a nice day, but a guide is essential to really bring the history of the place to life.

 When? Avoid the heat of the day in the summer and rain anytime. The *Oasi di Porto* is open to the public only from October until June. Check first to see if both parks are open, which may be particularly likely on Thursdays.

FUN FACTS

❋ There was a palace at Portus that provided dignitaries a place to prepare themselves for upcoming journeys or a place to recover from long
   boat trips before returning to Rome.

❋ Unlike the military ships of ancient Rome, which were primarily
   propelled by multiple levels of oars rowed by enslaved people, the
   merchant fleet predominantly used wind power. Roman merchant ships
   were also large for their time, with cargo capacity not equaled until the
   16th century AD.

*Enrichment: The Portus Necropolis on Isola Sacra is only a short car ride
away and provides a fascinating FREE look at how the families of the 1st
to 4th centuries treated their dead. Also check out Ostia Antica and the
Civic Museum of the Sea and Ancient Navigation in Santa Severa (both
adventures in this book) for more information about the importance of sea
transportation to ancient Rome.*

In the Roman neighborhood of Testaccio sits Monte dei Cocci, *a mound
of amphora shards accumulated from about 150 bc to 250 ad that currently
covers 2 hectares and stands 35 meters high. Amphorae are clay pots
that ancient Romans used to transport liquids like oil and wine from the
far reaches of their empire. Amphora were single-use vessels that were
systematically discarded once their cargo was delivered to market. It is
estimated that the mound contains the shards of 53 million amphorae.
It is possible to climb "Monte Testaccio" with prior arrangement.*

www.ostiaantica.beniculturali.it/en/archaeological-sites-and-monuments
/imperial-harbours-of-claudius-and-trajan/

www.oasidiporto.eu/index.html

www.portusproject.org

The Aqueduct Park

What is cooler than a Roman aqueduct? With over a million people living a relatively water-intensive lifestyle in ancient Rome (so many baths!), there had to be a great supply of the wet stuff. Aqueducts were structures built by Roman engineers to let gravity bring freshwater from the springs and lakes in the surrounding hills into the city. There were 11 aqueducts into ancient Rome, including the 6 that began in the Albani Hills to the southeast and now pass through the Aqueduct Park. The first one was completed in 312 BC and the last in 226 AD. Though the preferred conveyance of water was underground to protect it from evaporation and scavenging, using gravity necessitated building vast bridges for water to pass over low-lying areas.

Why go? The Aqueduct Park has 7 unique aqueducts, including one that is underground and the *Acqua Felice* aqueduct, which was built in 1586 and still conveys water today. On a clear day it is possible to see the Albani Hills on the horizon, the source of much of the water, and imagine it flowing into the city. *Via Latina*, an ancient Roman Road that heads east toward the same hills and is made of flat paving stones, also passes through the park.

 Where? The Aqueduct Park is roughly 8 kilometers southeast of Centro at the edge of urban Rome. The easiest way to get there is on the A Line toward Anagnina. Get off at the *Giulio Agricola* stop then head south for four blocks.

 Cost and time? The park is FREE and it will take a couple of hours to walk around and see the various aqueducts and the paving stones of *Via Latina*.

 Kids? Aqueduct Park is well-used by locals to play, picnic, exercise, and hang out. It's a city park that happens to have some

really cool history. All kids will have a fun time there as there are playgrounds and occasionally pony rides.

 Guide? The park itself offers a pleasant walk on a nice day, but if you really want to learn about the aqueducts and the ancient road, hire a guide.

 When? Anytime that you would go to an outdoor park is a good time to go the Aqueduct Park. Bring a picnic!

FUN FACTS

* Some of the buildings that were built near the aqueducts after the fall of the Roman Empire cannibalized materials from the aqueducts themselves. You may notice that where there is an old villa, there is also a gap in the aqueduct ruins.
* One of the reasons there wasn't more development in the area of the park was its long history as a malaria-infested wetland (don't worry, it's not anymore).
* Aqueduct Park hosts an outdoor cinema in the summertime, which features movies filmed at nearby Cinecittà Studios (#LX).

≡ www.parcodegliacquedotti.it

ADVENTURE #X

Catacombs of Rome

The catacombs of Rome are underground cemeteries that were primarily active between the 2nd and 5th centuries AD. As the pagan practice of
cremation gave way to the Jewish and Christian practices of burial, communal burial chambers were built deeper and deeper underground due
to the high demand for urban real estate. Over 60 catacombs have been
identified in Rome, usually along the ancient, paved roads leading outside
the city walls. Some of these intricate labyrinths of cave-like passageways
stretch for many kilometers and have several levels. Corpses were usually
placed in individual niches that were covered with marbled gravestones.
In the intervening centuries, grave robbers and opportunists desecrated
many of these sites in search of valuables, and few bones exist in their
intended resting places today. The Vatican oversees the Christian catacombs, and currently six of them are open to the public. There are also six
known Jewish catacombs, of which only two (*Vigna Randanini* and *Villa
Torlonia*) still exist and are open for visitors with prior special arrangement.

Why go? Apart from the dark subject matter, the catacombs are an interesting historical, social, spiritual, and spelunking experience. From elaborate family chambers to individual cubbies and from regal pillars to dead-
end alleyways, there is a wide range of burial enclosures. All the catacombs

are unique and worth a visit. Most likely you won't see bodies and bones, since most of them have long dissolved with age. But for goodness' sake, don't go if you're claustrophobic!

 Where? The six Christian catacombs open to the public are:

1. Saint Sebastian is on *Via Appia*, accessible via the 118 bus which goes out from the city center and stops in front of this church. There are both pagan and Christian sections in this catacomb.

2. Saint Callixtus is also on *Via Appia*, about a kilometer closer to Centro. This is the biggest catacomb with roughly 20 kilometers of corridors.

3. Domitilla is on *Via delle Sette Chiese*, not far from either Saint Sebastian or Saint Callixtus. There are 17 kilometers of catacombs inside and picnic tables outside.

4. Priscilla is on *Via Salaria*. The 63 and 92 buses stop about a block away. The catacombs contain a painting of one of the earliest depictions of the nativity with wise men.

5. Saint Agnes is on *Via Nomentana* and is very close to the Sant'Agnese/Annibaliano subway stop on the B1 Line. This is one of the lesser-visited catacombs and is walking distance to Priscilla.

6. Saint Marcellino and Saint Peter is on *Via Casilina*, along which the FC1 tram runs from Rome-Termini station. Apart from the niches, it is most known for its paintings and Helena's mausoleum next door.

 Cost and time? Entry to the Christian catacombs will cost €8/ adult, but kids under 6 are FREE. Tours usually take about an hour, and typically leave every 30 to 60 minutes.

 Kids? Little kids will find catacombs pretty creepy, both for the subject matter and the close proximity of the walls. And there is no allowance for strollers. Teens and tweens, however, might find the catacombs the highlight of their time in Rome.

 Guide? Yes, public entry into the catacombs is only allowed on a tour with a catacomb guide. They don't like people getting lost down there! The guides will organize visitors into appropriate language groups, including English. No photos are allowed in the catacombs.

 When? Anytime they are open. The catacombs near *Via Appia* seem to coordinate their opening times so that at least one is open every day. Save this adventure for a day when the weather isn't all that great. They are an excellent place to go on a hot day because the temperature underground is always cooler.

~~~~~~

FUN FACTS

* Prior to Christianity's arrival in Rome, burial was mostly based on social class. The wealthy were buried in grand mausoleums, the middle class were buried in much smaller mausoleums or were cremated, and the poor were buried in mass graves or wherever was convenient.

* The word catacomb means "next to the quarry", which indicates the first burials took advantage of existing excavations.

~~~~~~

Enrichment: *Most of the catacombs are associated with a church that will also be worth a visit. The Basilica of Saint Sebastian Outside the Walls, for instance, has a Bernini sculpture, and the Basilica of the Martyrs Nereus and Achilleus at Domitilla is one of the oldest churches in Rome. Sant'Agnese has the mausoleum of Costanza, the daughter of Emperor Constantine, who legalized Christianity in Rome in 313 AD.*

www.vatican.va/roman_curia/pontifical_commissions/archeo/inglese/documents/rc_com_archeo_doc_20011010_catacroma_en.html#Roma

www.catacombeditalia.va/content/archeologiasacra/en.html

Each catacomb also has its own website, not listed here.

ADVENTURE #XI

Villa dei Quintili

Built by the wealthy Quintili brothers, Valerius and Condianus, in the middle of the 2nd century AD, the regal and expansive *Villa dei Quintili* had baths, a nympheum, a hippodrome, an amphitheater, a multi-denominational worship chapel, and even its own branch of an aqueduct to feed its water demand. The villa was constructed at the 5th mile of the Appian Way, which at the time was considered to be way out in the suburbs of Rome. The villa was maybe too nice, however, because Emperor and megalomaniac Commodus had the brothers killed in 182 and snatched the villa for himself. The villa fell to succeeding emperors until finally falling into disrepair in the 6th century. Archeological excavations at the site began in the late 18th century, but they were originally more about the plunder of the booty than the telling of an historic tale. The excavation site was so large that it was referred to as *Roma Vecchia* (Old Rome). Today, the villa is part of the extensive Appia Antica Archeological Park and the ruins

are open to the public. It is situated on a hill between *Via Appia Antica* and *Via Appia Nuova*.

Why go? Though technically still in Rome, going to *Villa dei Quintili* is literally a walk in a grassy meadow park. Slightly off the beaten path (also quite literally), the ruins of the villa do not attract hordes of tourists, which can be a tempting respite from other Roman experiences. The ruins are picturesquely located on a hill, which is particularly beautiful at sunset. The primary visible structures are the baths, a gladiator training amphitheater, and floor mosaics. There is a small museum on the *Via Appia Nuova* side, and an ancient nympheum on the *Via Appia Antica* side.

Where? *Villa dei Quintili* is 9 kilometers southeast of *Piazza Venezia*. The villa can be accessed from either *Via Appia Antica* or *Via Appia Nuova*. The 85 bus gets you part of the way from *Piazza Venezia*, and then the 664 bus goes the rest of the way along *Via Appia Nuova*. Renting bicycles on the Appian Way is an excellent way to arrive at *Villa dei Quintili*.

Cost and time? Many of the sites along the Appian Way, including *Villa dei Quintili*, have coordinated a common entrance fee. It costs €10/adult, plus a €2 reservation fee, and is good for a year. It will take a couple of hours to explore the ruins.

Kids? Yes, the villa is nice mix of history and walking in a park.

Guide? Absolutely, it would be great to hear what it was like to live in this villa as the Quintilis intended during its peak, and to also hear more details on the upsetting lives of the Emperors from that period.

When? The ruins are exposed to the elements, so go when the weather is good. Traffic-free Sundays on the Appian Way are best for walking and bicycling. Other days are good along the road after about mile 4.

FUN FACTS

✳ The Quintili brothers were certainly not the only people that Emperor Commodus terrorized. During his period of leadership, he was at the center of the soap opera of intrigue and betrayals that the Roman Empire is known for. His megalomania culminated in him renaming Rome and all of the calendar months after himself. Commodus survived numerous assassination attempts until his enemies were ultimately successful in 192, when both his mistress and gladiator coach finally finished the job.

✳ Continuing the lunacy, the year after Commodus died was "The Year of Five Emperors." This is not to be confused with "The Year of Four Emperors" (69 AD) or "The Year of Six Emperors" (238 AD).

✳ Joaquin Phoenix played Commodus in the *Gladiator* movie (2000). Though he captured some of the craziness that Commodus must have exhibited, the movie was not a completely truthful rendition of actual events.

Enrichment: *There are many other ancient sites worth visiting along the Appian Way, including churches, catacombs, and mausoleums. There are also cafés and restaurants along the road, including the traditional* Osteria Qui Nun Se More Mai *(translated to "Here, you never die"). The Aqueduct Park and Cinecittà Studios are also not far away. Hadrian's Villa, outside of Tivoli, is another interesting glimpse at an imperial residence.*

www.parcoarcheologicoappiaantica.it/luoghi/villa-dei-quintili-e-santa
-maria-nova/

Hadrian's Villa in Tivoli

Hadrian's Villa (*Villa Adriana*) was the large country retreat of Emperor Hadrian at the beginning of the 2nd century AD. He disliked Rome enough that the villa eventually became his full-time home, at least when he wasn't touring the empire. The site included residences, baths, gardens, fountains, theaters, and temples. Almost two thousand people likely lived here to support the vast infrastructure. Hadrian was Emperor from 117 to 138, but Rome's elite used the villa until the end of the 3rd century, when it fell into a long decline concurrent with the fortunes of the Roman Empire. Outside of modern-day Tivoli, the villa complex now contains the ruins of over 30 building complexes covering 120 hectares, of which only 40 hectares are open to the public. It is a UNESCO World Heritage Site.

Why go? This is one of the "must-see" Roman ruins outside of Rome. Though much of the original structure and art are long gone (there are over 500 artifacts from Hadrian's Villa in the Vatican Museums), the size and opulence of the "little city" are still readily apparent. Water played an important role in this villa, which can still be seen in the *Canopus*, a statue- and column-lined pool, the *Poecile*, a garden with a large pool, and the Maritime Theater, with its circular moat where the Emperor might have gone for some peace and tranquility. Imagine the villa with beautiful sculptures modeled after the Greeks and Egyptians and elaborately stunning marble and mosaics.

 Where? Hadrian's Villa is 25 kilometers east-northeast of central Rome, and 3 kilometers southwest of present-day Tivoli. It is easiest to drive there, but there are also frequent buses to the villa from Tivoli (€1.30), which is easy to reach by train from Rome-Termini.

 Cost and time? The entrance fee to the villa grounds is €10/adult. There is also a small visitor center. Once you're here, the whole adventure should take at least several hours.

 Kids? Kids will love to imagine what it was like to live amongst the ruins and pools, but there is a decent amount of walking to get around.

 Guide? As there are many stories to be heard about the structures at Hadrian's Villa, you will appreciate the site much more with a guide. Did you know that Hadrian was passionate about architecture?

 When? Since the villa experience is entirely outside, good weather days are best.

FUN FACTS

✳ There was a labyrinth of tunnels under the villa (not open to the public) so that goods and servants could move about without being seen.

✳ Many country villas of that period were constructed on hilltops for security from invaders, but the high demand for water for the various pools and fountains required closer proximity to the low-elevation aqueducts bringing water to Rome.

✳ Hadrian completed the dome of the Pantheon (with the same diameter as the Maritime Theater) and built his namesake wall on the British frontier.

✳ In the 16th century, much of the remaining statues and marble from Hadrian's Villa were cannibalized by the builders of *Villa d'Este*, which is only 3 kilometers away.

Enrichment: Memoirs of Hadrian, *a novel by Marguerite Yourcenar, can provide interesting background information about the man and the place, and creates an atmosphere of what it must have been like to live as an emperor in that time.*

www.levillae.com/en/

www.villaadriana.beniculturali.it

www.visittivoli.eu/le-ville/villa-adriana&lang=EN

Lucus Feroniae

The Sacred Grove dedicated to the goddess Feronia (*Lucus Feroniae*) was a site revered by ancient Sabines as far back as the 7th century BC. Plundered of its religious and financial wealth by Hannibal in 211 BC, it was later developed as a colony for veterans of Caesar Augustus' reign in the early 1st century AD. It became an agricultural center until the 4th century, when the village was slowly abandoned. Today, *Lucus Feroniae* is an indoor and outdoor archaeological museum that contains the ruins of a 5,000-seat amphitheater, baths, and *Villa dei Volusii*, a residential complex with beautiful mosaics and small cells documented as enslaved people's quarters.

Why go? Though the forest grove is long gone, the archaeological museum is well worth the trip out of town, or as a stop on the way to adventures farther north. There are basically three parts to *Lucus Feroniae*: the small museum, the ruins of the main village, and the ruins of *Villa dei Volusii*. The museum has a unique large bas-relief depicting gladiators. The ruins of the village depict a market forum that sprang up adjacent to a large temple, and *Villa dei Volusii*, dating from the late Republican Age and at the edge of town, has beautiful floor mosaics and its own story to tell.

 Where? *Lucus Feroniae* is 28 kilometers northeast of central Rome, and it will take about 45 minutes to drive there. It is very convenient to the A1 motorway because the *Villa dei Volusii* is literally partially underneath it. The villa was rediscovered during the highway construction in 1961. It is not only situated adjacent to a highway exit, but also to one of the elevated highway rest stops. It's a great place to stop on your way to Florence!

Su concessione della Soprintendenza Archeologia Belle Arti e Paesaggio per la provincia di Viterbo e per l'Etruria meridionale

 Cost and time? The museum is FREE. It should take a couple of hours to see everything, and you can always combine your stop with a meal at the Autogrill, Italy's ubiquitous rest stop convenience stores.

 Kids? Absolutely, most of the museum is outside and it's small enough that no one should get bored.

Guide? Yes, there is a lot to unpack for such a small place, from the attraction of the namesake forest grove, to why Hannibal thought it worthy of pillage, to its heyday as a market destination.

When? The ruins of the village are open to the elements, but a roof protects most of the *Villa dei Volusii*. Some of the awesome floor mosaics can be covered with soil from October to March, however, to protect them from winter. The museum is closed on Mondays.

FUN FACTS

* Feronia is the ancient Roman goddess of the untamed, which encompasses wilderness, wildlife, and enslaved people who have been freed.
* Some of the museum statues have interchangeable parts. New emperor? No problem, just take the head with a likeness of the old emperor off and put the head of the new emperor on.
* The workers that rediscovered the bas-relief while excavating for a nearby house originally tried to sell it on the black market before being caught by the financial police (*Guardia di Finanza*).

Enrichment: *The Villa of Livia and Tusculum (also in this book) are other ancient ruins outside of Rome that were active at roughly the same time period as* Lucus Feroniae. *If you're interested in making your own mosaics, there are a couple of art studios in Rome that can help you (see websites below).*

www.etruriameridionale.beniculturali.it/index.php?en/149/lucus-feroniae
-museum

www.aegeamosaici.jimdofree.com

www.michelangeloforaday.com

Tusculum

Tusculum was an ancient Latin city, dating from at least the 7th century BC, situated on one of the outer hills of the Alban volcano. The people of Tusculum had a pesky relationship with ancient Rome, but they were eventually the first Latin city to be granted Roman citizenship in 381 BC. The town became a resort for wealthy Romans, including Cicero, the great political thinker. Tusculum remained active even after the fall of the Roman Empire and became an early medieval stronghold, complete with a castle. By the 10th century Tusculum was again a thorn in the side of the Commune of Rome, and the Roman army finally destroyed it in 1191. Today, the ruins of Tusculum are within hiking distance of the *Castelli Romani* town of Frascati.

Why go? Tusculum's long history means that the origins of the ruins span many centuries, symbolized by a pre-Christian temple to a medieval basilica, and by a 2,000-seat amphitheater to the citadel on the hill. There is a market forum, a Roman road, a water system for the baths, and artistic floor mosaics. There are also nice views south into the valley and all the way to the sea. The ruins of Tusculum are part of the Castelli Romani Regional Park, which is roughly 15,000 hectares of forests, meadows, agricultural lands, and lakes, and includes 15 villages. You can even choose to include a walk in the park woods on your visit.

 Where? Tusculum is 22 kilometers southeast of central Rome, and less than 3 kilometers from Frascati, as the crow flies. It will take about an hour to drive there from Rome, or you can take the train to Frascati and walk or taxi from there. The hike will take about 40 minutes. It's only about a 500-meter walk from the car park to the ruins.

 Cost and time? The ruins are not extensive and can be viewed in an hour if you are looking for a quick outing. But if you choose to bring a picnic or combine your visit with a hike in the park, then your visit can be as long as you wish. Entrance to the ruins is €3/adult, but the hiking is FREE.

 Kids? This adventure is an outdoor walk in the forested hills with nice views and historic ruins thrown in for good measure. There are picnic tables adjacent to the car park. It's an excellent afternoon adventure!

 Guide? Yes, a lot went on in this small village over a long period of time. A guide will bring the excellent stories to life and connect them with what you may already know about Rome. A guided tour costs €5/adult and should be reserved in advance. Kids under 6 are FREE.

 When? Tusculum is only open on weekends or on weekdays for groups with reservations. Check the website before setting out. Since Tusculum is exposed to the elements on a hillside, avoid the heat of the day in the summer. On sunny weekend afternoons during other seasons, many picnickers frequent the grassy hillside.

FUN FACTS

✳ Gregory I, the Count of Tusculum from around 954 to 1012 AD, granted lands in the town of Grottaferatta to Nilus the Younger (a.k.a St. Nilo) for the construction of a monastery. See Adventure #XXIV.

✳ Imagine angering someone so much that they invaded and utterly destroyed every last structure in your whole town . . . and then no one even attempted to rebuild it for over 800 years. Those are some pretty bad vibes!

Enrichment: There are other "lost cities" in Lazio, including Castro, Santa Maria di Galeria, and Canale Monterano.

☰ www.tuscolo.org

Villa of Livia at Prima Porta

Livia Drusilla was the long-time third wife of the first emperor of Rome, Caesar Augustus. They were married for 52 years, which is extraordinary in an age when life expectancy was only 50 to 60 years. She lived from 58 BC until 29 AD. She brought her namesake villa into her second marriage (to Augustus), likely acquired as dowry from her first husband. Livia and Augustus used it as a country retreat to be closer to nature and their gardens. Of course, there were baths to stay cool in the summer and warm in the winter, and beautifully frescoed walls and mosaic floors. Today, the ruins of *Villa di Livia* are protected as a museum by the Ministry of Culture and are open to the public.

Why go? The Villa of Livia is most famous for the fresco trompe l'oeil of a verdant garden in the sunken dining room. While staying cool underground in the summertime, the occupants could still be reminded that they were in the country. The frescoes have been moved to the National Roman Museum at *Palazzo Massimo* in Rome, but the ruins of the villa are still fascinating to the connoisseur of Roman history. There is also a little museum on site.

 Where? The Villa of Livia is only 12 kilometers north *Piazza Venezia*. The *Prima Porta* train station is 300 meters away from the villa.

 Cost and time? The site is FREE, except for a €2 reservation fee. It should take about two hours to see the villa, depending on your interest.

 Kids? This is not one of the more kid-friendly adventures in this book. The kid's favorite part of this adventure may be the train ride to get there.

 Guide? Absolutely. This is not an easy site to appreciate without a guide.

 When? Much of the ruins are covered by a roof, providing shade from the sun and protection from the rain. Check their website for opening times (which are complicated).

~~~~~~

FUN FACTS

✳ Livia was also the mother of Emperor Tiberius (by her first marriage), the grandmother of Emperor Claudius, great-grandmother of Emperor Caligula, and great-great-grandmother of Emperor Nero, where the hereditary line tragically ended.

✳ Livia's villa was once called the Villa of the White Hens after a dream she had about an eagle dropping a white chicken in her lap with a sprig of laurel in its beak. Forever after she kept white chickens and grew

laurel in the garden of the villa. Dreaming of white chickens suggests new adventures in life, and laurel is a symbol of victory.

✳ *Prima Porta,* or First Door, is named after an arch in the aqueduct that brought water to the Villa of Livia. It was the first indication to travelers that they had reached ancient Rome.

Enrichment: Not only are the beautiful frescoes from the Villa of Livia now on display at the National Roman Museum at Palazzo Massimo *in Rome, but the famous statue* Augustus of Prima Porta, *also found at the Villa of Livia, is now displayed at the Vatican Museums. You can also visit Livia's city house,* Casa di Livia, *on Palatine Hill. There are many books written about Livia, both nonfiction and fictionalized, if you'd like to know more about her. The Arch of Malborghetto, commemorating the victory of Constantine over Emperor Maxentius in 312 AD, is 6 kilometers north of* Villa di Livia.

www.soprintendenzaspecialeroma.it/schede/villa-di-livia_3027/

www.soprintendenzaspecialeroma.it/schede/arch-of-malborghetto_3011/

Villa of Tiberius at Sperlonga

Emperors also like beach vacations! Tiberius was the 2nd Roman emperor, from 14 to 37 AD, and he chose this spot for his beachside getaway no doubt because of the large grotto around which the villa was constructed ("Sperlonga" means "cave" in Latin). He used to entertain around the cooling pools in the grotto, which were lined by amazing sculptures, including a giant reclining Cyclops character made famous by Homer's epic poem *The Odyssey*. Unfortunately, Tiberius was almost killed when the cave partially collapsed in the year 26, and successive cave-ins eventually reduced many of the sculptures to pieces. Today, the ruins of the villa and the grotto are part of the Archaeological Museum of Sperlonga, which includes reproductions of some of the grotto sculptures.

Why go? Located at the eastern end of East Sperlonga Beach, which is 1.2 kilometers long and peppered with beach clubs, the Villa of Tiberius combines 2,000-year-old history with a beautiful beach day. Go to the villa museum in the summer and then rent a chair and umbrella on the beach. Go in the winter and have the beach all to yourself. The sea at Sperlonga is known for its clear water.

Where? The town of Sperlonga is 108 kilometers southeast of Rome. It's easiest to get there by car but there is also a train station 10 kilometers away from the ruins at Fondi-Sperlonga. A bus from the station will get you to Sperlonga.

Cost and time? Entrance for an adult is €5. Seeing the museum, villa, and grotto will take a couple of hours. Relaxing at the beach could take all summer!

 Kids? Yes, combining history with a visit to the beach is great for the whole family. And the grotto is pretty cool, especially imagining the banquets that it could have hosted back in the day. Kids will also love Homer's tales of Odysseus' adventures.

 Guide? Yes, a guide will be able to make the villa come alive. A Roman guide can join you on a day trip, with the beach included, but there are local guides too.

When? Summertime is the best time to go to the Villa of Tiberius if you want to combine it with the Italian beach experience. Wintertime is better if you want a cooler and quieter adventure. For some, the empty windswept vista on a winter day is perfection.

FUN FACTS

* After the grotto collapse, Tiberius moved on to *Villa Jovis* on the island of Capri to further avoid life in Rome.
* The ruins of the Villa of Tiberius were rediscovered in 1957 when the coast road was being constructed.

Enrichment: *Reading passages from Homer's* Odyssey *will give context to the statues. If you are interested in tasting wine made from ancient grape varieties, the Monti Cecubi Winery (#LXXVI) is only 6 kilometers from Sperlonga. There are many other beaches along the road, so don't feel like you need to stay on the one preferred by Tiberius.*

www.polomusealelazio.beniculturali.it/index.php?en/172/the
-archaeological-museum-of-sperlonga

The Middle Ages

Crypta Balbi

Don't let the name fool you, *Crypta Balbi* is not another subterranean tour of gravesites. Instead, this modern museum is a chronicle of one city block in the center of Rome, from ancient times through the Middle Ages and the Renaissance. The name refers to a dark backstage area of a 6,500-seat amphitheater built on the site in 13 BC by Lucius Cornelius Balbus. The museum highlights the temporal transition of the place, from the ancient theater to a functioning medieval quartier of craftsmen to a 17th-century convent. There are active excavations through multiple levels in the basement and the courtyard, two floors of permanent exhibits including fascinating maps, and one floor of special installations.

Why go? *Crypta Balbi* is unlike any other museum in Rome. It provides a new perspective by documenting the evolution of a small space through the long strata of time. There are countless artifacts upstairs that were excavated from downstairs, and endless stories to go with them.

 Where? The *Crypta Balbi* is less than 400 meters southwest of *Piazza Venezia* on *Via delle Botteghe Oscure*.

 Cost and time? The *Crypta Balbi* is one of the four locations of the National Roman Museum, the others being *Palazzo Massimo*, *Palazzo Altemps*, and the Baths of Diocletian. A €12 ticket will get you into all four sites and is valid for a week. *Crypta Balbi* is not large, but it can take a couple of hours to explore, especially if you have an exciting guide.

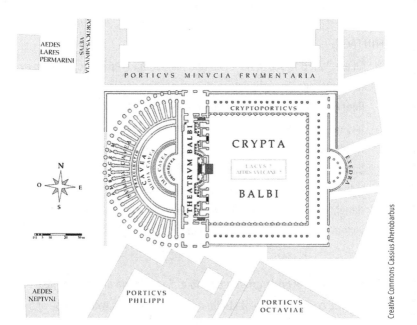

Kids? As for many museums not geared toward children, younger kids will need your help to stay engaged. Perhaps have a sketch-pad or activity book with an ancient Rome theme?

Guide? Yes, there is a lot going on in this museum that will generally be lost on the many tourists passing by quickly (there is a lot to be seen in this neighborhood). A guide can pull subtle information from the many pieces of this museum into a more cogent temporal story.

When? It's mostly an indoor museum, so go on a day when the weather isn't great. The archeological excavations in the basement and in the courtyard are not always open, so check the website and be sure to go when you can see them.

FUN FACTS

* An excavated fresco in the museum, painted and repainted at three distinct times through history, dramatizes the rise in the height of the floor over time since all of the paintings display the subjects' feet at the base of that period's fresco. The feet in the oldest fresco are roughly 0.5 meter lower than those in the repainting several centuries later, and another half of a meter lower than the newest fresco.

* In the 16th century, the convent at this site became a shelter for the daughters of prostitutes, who would be put on public "display" twice a year in hopes of attracting a husband.

Enrichment: *The underground church at* Santa Maria in Via Lata, *just around the corner from* Crypta Balbi *on* Via del Corso, *is where some of the frescoes at* Crypta Balbi *originated. The only other museum in Rome dedicated to the Middle Ages is the* Museo delle Civiltà Romana *in EUR, which is currently closed.*

☰ www.museonazionaleromano.beniculturali.it/en/crypta-balbi/

Castel Sant'Angelo

It's a mausoleum, it's a stronghold, it's a castle, it's a refuge, it's a prison, it's a museum. Originally built as a regal mausoleum for Emperor Hadrian in 139 AD and topped with a statue of Hadrian himself in a chariot, it became the final resting place of many successive emperors and their families. By 275, the mausoleum had been incorporated into the Aurelian Walls to help protect Rome from invaders. It got its current name in 590, when Pope Gregory I had a vision of Archangel Michael sheathing his sword above the mausoleum, signaling the end of a ravaging plague. From the 10th to 14th centuries, the castle was the residence of various affluent Roman families. The *Passetto di Borgo* was built by Pope Nicholas III in 1277 as an elevated escape route from the Vatican to the castle, because he considered the castle more secure in times of invasion. Indeed, the bridge served its purpose at least twice over the centuries. Popes lived in the castle when it suited them and they continued to bolster its fortification for protection. They also made it into a prison, a function it served until 1901. Now it's one of the most popular museums in Rome.

Why go? From the majestic Empire to the violent sacking of Rome by the Visigoths to a medieval citadel to the Renaissance art of a Papal residence to a dark and tortuous prison to today's museum — there is nearly 2,000 years of Roman history in one building! The castle has seven levels, from the Courtyard of Executions on the 1st level to the Terrace of the Angel on the 7th level, which has amazing views. In between are niches for urns and sarcophagi, prison cells, munitions storage, barracks, Papal apartments, and the treasury. The tour is not necessarily in chronological order, but how could it be with so many things happening in the same space. The spiral ramp to the mausoleum is still impressive. The *Passetto* is fascinating but rarely open to the public. There is also a nice café with an awesome view.

 Where? *Castel Sant'Angelo* is only 1.5 kilometers northwest from the *Piazza Venezia*, between the Vatican and the Tiber River, about a 25-minute walk. If you walk along the river, you can't miss it. There are also a slew of buses that run from the *Piazza* along *Corso Vittorio Emanuele* to the castle.

 Cost and time? The cost to get into *Castel Sant'Angelo* is €15/adult but check for FREE days. It will take a couple of hours to get through the many layers of the castle.

 Kids? On one hand, the *Castel Sant'Angelo* packs the huge punch of so much Roman history in one building. This will be awesome for tweens and teens. But on the other hand, much of that history is quite dark, which will be challenging to many younger kids.

 Guide? Yes, of course. There are so many stories to be told about this place. They do rent audio guides inside the museum, however.

When? In the past, the first Sunday of every month was a good time to go to the castle because it was FREE, but due to the long lines to get inside, free days may now be discontinued (check the website). If you can time your ascension to the Terrace of the Angel at sunset you will not be disappointed. In the summer, the castle is open at night with reservations, often with entertainment in the courtyard.

FUN FACTS

✳ A statue of Saint Michael and his sword has been on top of the *Castello* since at least the 13th century.

✳ Pope Urban V agreed to return from France in 1367 during the Avignon Papacy, but only if he was given the keys to the castle, signifying that he was the most powerful person in Rome.

✳ The first fireworks in Rome, known as *La Girandola*, were launched from the *Castel Sant'Angelo* in 1481 in celebration of the feast for Saints Peter and Paul on June 29th. Today, *La Girandola* has moved to the Pincio Terrace above *Piazza del Popolo*.

✳ It's seldom open, but occasionally tours get to see the pope's bathroom.

Enrichment: To learn more about Hadrian, visit the ruins of his expansive villa outside of Tivoli. At the climax of Puccini's opera Tosca, *the title character throws herself from the ramparts of* Castel Sant'Angelo *(sorry to ruin it for you). Nearby to the castle is the Mausoleum of Augustus, which would have been similar to each other when they were first constructed. Augustus' mausoleum has only recently been reopened to the public.*

www.castelsantangelo.beniculturali.it
www.mausoleodiaugusto.it

Three Fountains Abbey

The Three Fountains Abbey (*Abbazia delle Tre Fontane*) is a Trappist monastery (i.e., Cistercian) on the outskirts of Rome. The story says that when St. Paul was decapitated during Emperor Nero's persecution of Christians in 67 AD, his head bounced on the ground three times creating the springs that fed the three fountains of the abbey. The first church was erected on the site in the 5th century AD, and the abbey continues to be a tranquil place.

Trappist monks generally believe in minimizing conversation, eating vegetarian, and living "by the work of their own hands." Over the last century or so, the monks at Three Fountains Abbey have rehabilitated much of their land through draining malaria-plagued areas and planting Japanese

Eucalyptus trees. They continue to produce much of what they need by farming, milling olive oil, and brewing beer (including some flavored with eucalyptus).

Why go? There are three churches to visit at the abbey, though much of the grounds are closed to the public. There is also a shop that sells goods produced by the monks, including olive oil, honey, and chocolate. The Three Fountains Abbey is one of only 14 breweries in the world that produce Trappist beer. To give the public a window into the life of a Trappist monk there is also a virtual tour of the abbey without ever leaving the shop, by using 3D glasses.

 Where? The Three Fountains Abbey is 7 kilometers south of Piazza Venezia. There is parking at the abbey, though you can also walk from both the EUR Fermi and Laurentina subway stops at the southern end of the B Line.

 Cost and time? Seeing the churches is FREE but coming home with some monk-produced goods is not. Prices are quite modest however.

 Kids? There may not be a lot here to keep the kids engaged beyond the promise of monk-made candy.

 Guide? The 3D virtual tour is almost like a real guide, but a "real" guide will be able to answer your questions.

 When? The churches and shop are open every day of the week.

FUN FACTS

✳ St. Paul may have died here, but he is buried at the Basilica of St. Paul Outside the Walls.

✳ It is rumored that 10,000 Christian enslaved people are buried in a hillside near the abbey.

Enrichment: It is possible to rent a room at the abbey as a spiritual retreat. The maximum stay is six days in exchange for an offering. Other Cistercian monasteries within easy driving distance from Rome include Casamari, Fossanova, and Valvisciolo (another adventure in this book). The fascist-style architecture of the buildings in the neighborhood of EUR, just outside the gates of the abbey, were built by Mussolini and worth a walking tour.

☰ www.abbaziatrefontane.it

ADVENTURE #XX

Sanctuary of Greccio

Saint Francis of Assisi organized the first-ever live nativity (i.e., real humans playing the roles) on Christmas Eve in 1223 in a grotto on a mountainside near the village of Greccio in the Rieti Valley. The site was soon developed into a Franciscan sanctuary, along with three other Franciscan shrines in *Valle Santa* (*Poggio Bustone*, *Fonte Colombo*, and *La Foresta*). The sanctuaries are now part of The St. Francis Way (*La Via di Francesco*), a multi-stage pilgrimage route following the footsteps of St. Francis from La Verna in the north and Rome in the south to the Basilica of St. Francis in the town of Assisi.

Why go? The sanctuary hangs on a mountainside with beautiful views of the valley. There is a chapel to commemorate the nativity, and frescoes from the 13th century. There is also a trail up *Monte San Francesco* to *La Cappelletta*, a hermitage where St. Francis went for solitude. It has stunning views as well.

 Where? The Sanctuary of Greccio is 67 kilometers northeast of Rome and 11 kilometers northwest of the city of Rieti. It will take about an hour and a half to drive there from Rome.

 Cost and time? The sanctuary, which is FREE, is quite small and it won't take long to see the chapel. It's about 6.5 kilometers to hike up the forested trail to *La Cappelletta*, which is also FREE.

 Kids? Sure, but there isn't a lot for the kids. If you're hiking, the elevation gain is about 600 meters, and though the hike isn't difficult, younger kids will find it hard. If your teenagers like nature, however, they will love it.

 Guide? St. Francis was a very interesting character and has obviously garnered much respect over the centuries. Getting immersed in the stories of his life through a guide would be fantastic, but this site alone does not warrant having a guide along.

 When? The best time for the views would be on a nice day. If you're going on the hike, make sure that the good weather window is suitably long enough for your return.

* Legend has it that a kid throwing a burning ember onto the hillside helped St. Francis to identify the spot where the nativity should be held.
* The inanimate baby Jesus in the nativity was said to have come to life during the reenactment only to become inanimate again afterward.

Enrichment: *When St. Francis came to Rome, he stayed several times at the convent associated with the* San Francesco a Ripa *church in Trastevere (so named after he became a saint). The church also has a Bernini sculpture. Obviously, exploring the life of St. Francis would not be complete without a visit to Assisi.*

www.viadifrancesco.it/en/

www.wikiloc.com/hiking-trails/la-cappelletta-dal-santuario-di-s-francesco -greccio-44865099#wp-44865104

ADVENTURE #XXI

The Abbey of Farfa

The Abbey of Farfa is a Benedictine monastery with a long, rich, and tumultuous history. Originally founded in the middle of the 6th century as a place of quiet retreat, it was soon destroyed by marauding Germanic Lombards. Rediscovered and rebuilt at the end of the 7th century, it was again sacked at the end of the 9th century, this time by Saracens (Arab Muslims). Rebuilt for a third time, it fell into mismanagement by delinquent monks who pilfered anything of value. By the end of the 10th century, however, Abbot Hugo found a recipe for success, and soon the monks of Farfa were devoted to intellectual pursuits and amassing wealth and power. At their peak, they owned hundreds of villages in the region, including castles, churches, mills, and mines. Eventually the wealth of Farfa became a perk for the families of the Pope. For over 200 years, the commendatory abbots (i.e., fiscal caretakers) of Farfa were from the Orsini, Farnese, and Barberini families. As Italy reformed over the last several centuries, Farfa's influence declined, but it still has an active monastery and a small medieval village.

Why go? The village and abbey at Farfa make for a nice afternoon getaway from Rome. The surrounding Sabina Hills provide a classic Italian driving experience, which culminates in this beautiful and quaint abbey, with cloisters, church frescoes, an historic library, and ruins of the 9th century

Luca Pietrosanti

church. The village is made up of just a few streets, with artisan shops and a popular restaurant. There is also an "Herbalist Shop" at the abbey that sells natural products like olive oil, soaps, honey, and liqueurs.

 Where? The Abbey of Farfa is roughly 40 kilometers northeast of Rome. It takes about an hour to drive there, or longer if you're not in a hurry and want to enjoy a ride in the country. A bus will get you there too, but you'll have to switch buses partway. There is a train station about 10 kilometers away in Passo Corese.

 Cost and time? Seeing the church and wandering the shops in the village are FREE.

 Kids? Little kids may not be that interested in the rise and fall of Farfa, but there's always gelato.

 Guide? There are guided tours of the abbey every day except Mondays. It costs €8/adult and the guide may or may not speak much English.

 When? The best time to go to Farfa is on a day when the driving is good (i.e., good weather or Sundays).

FUN FACTS

＊ The abbey was sacked for a third time in 1798, this time by the French.
＊ Today, the population of the village of Farfa is less than 50 people.

Enrichment: It's possible to stay at the abbey if you're looking for a religious retreat. There's also an interesting second-hand shop in Farfa. Not far from the abbey is Le Gole del Farfa, *a beautiful river gorge where you can hike and explore if canyoning (#C) appeals to you.*

☰ www.abbaziadifarfa.com

Church of San Pietro in Tuscania

The *Chiesa di San Pietro* is an 11th century Romanesque and Gothic-style church that still stands on the top of a hill in northern Lazio. The first church on the site (from the 8th century) likely predates the existing structure, and that one was built on the ruins of an Etruscan acropolis from at least the 5th century BC. The present church is known for its large rose window, floor mosaics, and surrounding fortified walls. There are also three defensive towers, which, along with the rest of the church buildings, suffered damage from an earthquake in 1971. Just down the hill is the Church of Santa Maria Maggiore, which was first documented in the 9th century.

Why go? Both churches are beautiful and classic examples of architecture from the Middle Ages, and they overlook a gorgeous valley with extensive history. The exterior façade of the Church of San Pietro includes statues of a bull, griffin, lion, and dragons chasing dogs. There is also an interesting bas-relief representing demons. The austerity of the interior of the church only adds to the medieval ambiance.

 Where? Tuscania is 76 kilometers northwest of Rome, and it takes about 90 minutes to get there by car. It's also possible to get there by patching together trains and buses.

 Cost and time? Both of the churches are FREE and visiting them will take a couple of hours. But check to make sure they're open before setting out.

 Kids? There isn't much specifically for the kids here, but the location helps dramatize the reach of the Church into the Italian countryside in the Middle Ages. And there's always the chance of a gelato in the town of Tuscania.

 Guide? Like all things historical, a local guide will be able to tell the stories that bring the place alive.

 When? The best time to go to Tuscania is whenever you are in the mood for wandering the northern Lazio countryside.

FUN FACTS

＊ Rose windows evolved from the oculus windows of ancient Rome (i.e., the top of the Pantheon). Originally developed to let more light into a dark interior space, by the Middle Ages they were also designed with religious symbolism.

＊ A plague in the middle of the 14th century resulted in the abandonment of the medieval village that surrounded the churches. The village fell into disrepair and was never rebuilt. The present village of Tuscania is slightly removed from the churches.

Enrichment: Many movies have been filmed at the church, including Franco Zeffirelli's Romeo and Juliet (1968). In the valley below the towers of San Pietro is the Etruscan Necropoli of Scalette. It dates back to the 7th century BC. You should also walk through the walled village of Tuscania, with cobblestone alleyways and churches around every corner. An adventure to Tuscania could be combined with a visit to the Papal Palace of Viterbo, which is about 20 kilometers west, or a visit to the Etruscan ruins of Vulci, which are about 20 kilometers east.

☰ www.comune.tuscania.vt.it/Basilica%20di%20San%20Pietro.php

ADVENTURE #XXIII

Cistercian Abbeys

There are three Cistercian Abbeys in southern Lazio that are very similar to each other and quite beautiful. Dating from the 12th and 13th centuries, the Casamari, Valvisciolo, and Fossanova Abbeys mixed aspects of northern European gothic architecture into Middle Ages monasteries across southern Italy. They are each centered, of course, around a church with handsome rose windows, and have adjacent tranquil cloisters and libraries. Their differences mainly arise from additions of frescoes in later centuries, namely at Valvisciolo. Since WWII, all the abbeys have been heavily restored. Each abbey is adjacent to pastoral agricultural lands and has a shop offering Cistercian-made goods.

Why go? The abbeys are aesthetically pleasing with unique architecture worth seeing, and each has a long history as a center of religious life and awareness. The Casamari Abbey also has a small museum. Typical goods found in the abbey shops include chocolate, jams, honey, cosmetics, beer, and liqueurs.

 Where? The three abbeys are between 55 and 85 kilometers southwest of Rome and are within about 40 kilometers of each other. Since they are secluded in the countryside, they are most easily reached by car. It will take about an hour and a half to drive to the Casamari Abbey from Rome.

Cost and time? Seeing the abbeys and their churches is FREE.

 Kids? Not really. There is not much that is geared toward children at the abbeys.

 Guide? Yes, and the Cistercian monks may be willing to discuss the history of their abbey between their other responsibilities.

 When? Anytime that you are in the mood for a drive through southern Lazio.

FUN FACTS

* Thomas Aquinas, the Dominican philosopher, died at the Fossanova Abbey in 1274.
* The rarest of the books from the abbey libraries have been moved to the Vatican.
* Trappists, another name for Cistercians, branched off from Benedictines with a stricter interpretation of their teachings.

Enrichment: *It is possible to stay at the Casamari Abbey, either as a pilgrim on the trails of* Cammino di San Benedetto *and* Via Francigena del Sud, *or on a religious retreat. If you don't want to drive all the way to Frosinone for your Cistercian* amaro, *a classically Italian herbal digestif, there's also a shop that has Trappist goods at the Three Fountains Abbey in the EUR neighborhood of Rome.*

www.abbaziadicasamari.it
www.abbaziadifossanova.it
www.museoabbaziavalvisciolo.it

ADVENTURE #XXIV

Abbey of San Nilo in Grottaferrata

Also known as the Abbey of Santa Maria, the Abbey of San Nilo was founded by Saint Nilus in the early 11th century and has thereafter been administered by Basilian monks who adhere to the traditional Greek liturgy. The abbey is famous for its Romanesque church that has late 11th-century wooden doors, above which are medieval mosaics. There is also a bell tower, gardens, a famous library, and surrounding fortifications from the 15th century. There are beautiful frescoes added by Domenichino during a renovation in the 17th century, and a small but interesting museum.

Why go? The Abbey of San Nilo is the last Greek Byzantine monastery in Italy. The architecture is a beautiful mix of styles and structures. From the outside, the abbey looks like a fortress; from the inside, the cloisters are peaceful and the medieval baptismal font is covered with a whimsical bas-relief. There is also an odd elevated and fortified room at the southern end of the ramparts that begs the question, "What is that for?" There is a small shop that sells San Nilo wine.

 Where? The abbey is located in the village of Grottaferrata in the *Castelli Romani*, 20 kilometers southeast of central Rome. It will take about half an hour to drive there or you can take the train to Frascati and catch the local bus.

 Cost and time? There is a small fee to get into the abbey museum, but otherwise seeing the abbey is FREE. Make sure the museum is open before you go.

 Kids? The fortified abbey has a classic medieval look, and the views from the walls are quite nice. But there isn't anything particularly interesting for younger kids. There is good gelato and pizza, however, just across the street, and an *agriturismo* restaurant with a petting zoo 500 meters northwest of the abbey.

 Guide? Yes, the history of the abbey is particularly interesting because of the unique presence of a Byzantine monastery so close to Rome.

 When? Go anytime you have a spare morning or afternoon and want to get out of town.

FUN FACTS

✳ The abbey was built upon the ruins of an ancient Roman villa.

✳ The view from the top of the walls spans from Rome to the sea.

✳ The icon of the abbey, which is kept in the church, is a wooden board painted with an image of the Virgin Mary and probably rescued from Tusculum (#XIV).

Enrichment: *The nearby towns are famous for wine (Frascati) and porchetta (Ariccia). The lost city of Tusculum is less than 4 kilometers from the abbey as the crow flies, and the histories of Tusculum and the San Nilo Abbey are linked with common threads (the Count of Tusculum granted the land for the abbey to Saint Nilus).*

≡ www.abbaziagreca.it

Subiaco Monastery

Long before Benedict became the patron saint of Europe, he was a thoughtful 6th century guy looking for some peace and quiet in the mountains east of Rome. He found a cave outside the village of Subiaco where he lived as a hermit for three years. Once he emerged, his growing reputation as a charismatic spiritual guide drew enough followers that he eventually founded 12 monasteries in the area around the town. Today, only two of the original abbeys are still active: Monastery of Saint Benedict and the Monastery of Saint Scholastica. The Monastery of Saint Benedict hangs on a mountainside and encompasses St. Benedict's original hermitage cave. The Monastery of Saint Scholastica, named after St. Benedict's twin sister, is less than a kilometer away and shares a common Benedictine community.

Both abbeys were rebuilt after being sacked by Saracens (Arab Muslims) in the 9th century and currently contain a mix of buildings from the 11th century onward.

Why go? Both abbeys overlook the steep and picturesque Aniene River valley. The Saint Benedict Abbey contains the *Santuario del Sacro Speco*, or the sacred cave of Benedict's hermitage. It also contains beautiful frescoes including the oldest known portrait of St. Francis, without a halo, likely painted between when he died (1226) and when he was canonized (1228). The Saint Scholastica Abbey has a well-known library and three peaceful cloisters, each with its own architectural style. The monks also run a guesthouse with an accompanying restaurant and have a shop that sells natural products such as honey, jam, tea, cosmetics, and liqueurs.

 Where? The village of Subiaco is 52 kilometers east of Rome, and it should take less than 90 minutes to drive there. There is also a bus from the Rome-Tiburtina station that goes directly to Subiaco for about €8 each way.

Cost and time? The two abbeys are FREE. Both are relatively small and should take a couple of hours to see.

 Kids? Teens will be able to appreciate the history and beauty of the place, but there isn't much of interest for the younger kids. Maybe bring an empty notebook and help them create and illustrate their own story.

 Guide? The monks of the abbeys do FREE tours in both Italian and English. You may be expected, however, to leave an appropriate donation.

 When? Anytime is the right time to go the Subiaco Monastery. They are closed every day for siesta, from 12:15 to 15:30.

FUN FACTS

✳ The Saint Scholastica Monastery was the site of Italy's first printing house when two disciples of Johannes Gutenburg brought new printing press technology from Germany in 1465. This made hand-written and hand-illustrated books obsolete.

✳ In the 1st century, Emperor Nero dammed the Aniene River in three places to create three artificial lakes. On one of the lakes, he built a magnificent country villa, which became known as *Sublaqueum*, meaning "under the lake." "Subiaco" is a derivation of the name of Nero's villa. The lakes were still present in Benedict's time, but the dams were eventually destroyed by flooding in 1305.

Enrichment: *The pilgrimage trail of St. Benedict passes through Subiaco, starting from Benedict's birthplace in the village of Norcia in the north, to the Abbey of Montecassino in the south where he died. There are many guidebooks specifically about the St. Benedict and St. Francis trails. It is possible to see the ruins of Nero's* Sublaqueum *and imagine the three artificial lakes. A local river rafting company,* Vivere l'Aniene, *runs trips on* *the Aniene River from their base in Subiaco (#XCIX). There is also a swim-ming hole,* Laghetto di San Benedetto, *in the valley bottom. The swimming "hole" is actually a natural pool below a beautiful waterfall and the water is always cold, even in August. But it is so popular that on summer week-ends access can be restricted.*

www.benedettini-subiaco.org
www.camminodibenedetto.it

Anagni Cathedral

The Anagni Cathedral is a Romanesque church that dates to the 11th cen-tury. It is known for its beautiful bell tower, the Cosmati-style floor mosaics (similar to the floors made by the famous Cosmati family), and the color-ful medieval frescoes in the low-ceilinged crypt, many illustrating martyr-dom stories. The Cathedral was at its peak in the 13th century when four men born in Anagni became pope, including three from the Conti family. The fourth pope from Anagni, Pope Boniface VIII, built his papal palace adjacent to the church. That palazzo was later used as a summer palace by many popes until the 17th century, when the palace at Castel Gandolfo was built. Today, the Anagni Cathedral has an accompanying museum, and together with the Palace of Boniface VIII, they are open to the public.

Why go? The town of Anagni sits atop a hill that provides beautiful views of the surrounding valleys. The overlook from the cathedral is particularly stunning. The buildings and museums provide an interesting window into the life and times of the medieval papacy, both as the city of popes (away from Rome, anyway) and for turbulent politics. There are also some spec-tacular rooms in both the cathedral and the palace.

 Where? The town of Anagni is 60 kilometers east-southeast of Rome. It takes about an hour to drive there. A bus goes from Rome-Tiburtina to Anagni a couple of times a day for about €5 each way.

 Cost and time? Like most churches in Italy, the Cathedral is FREE. The entry fee for the Cathedral museum, however, is €9 for an adult. It will take at least an hour see all the rooms in the museum. They keep people moving through the crypt by turning off the lights after 20 minutes. The cost to get into the Boniface Palace is €5 and should also take about an hour. It's FREE for kids under 12.

 Kids? The church and the palace are classically medieval. Teens and tweens should be able to appreciate the intrigue of the historic time and the beauty of the place.

Guide? You can visit the cathedral with your own guide or they can provide a guide for you. The cost depends on the number of people in your party. The entry fee for the Palace of Boniface VIII includes an audio guide.

When? Anytime you are looking to get out of Rome to see something new. Much of this adventure is inside so it would be suitable for mediocre weather day.

~~~~~~

FUN FACTS

✳ Boniface VIII's papal career was a bit of a disaster. His power struggle with the King of France, Phillip the Fair, precipitated the king to send troops to Anagni in 1303. The combative pope was taken prisoner, but legend says not before being slapped in his own palace by one of the invaders with his armored glove. This episode became known as the *Schiaffo di Anagni*, or the Slap of Anagni.

✳ To make matters worse for an Italian papacy, when a Frenchman (Clement V) became pope two years later, he moved the papal enclave away from Rome to Avignon, France, where it stayed for the next 67 years.

~~~~~~

Enrichment: The ruins of Villa Magna, an imperial villa of unknown origin but certainly dating from at least the end of 1st century AD, is only 8 kilometers from the town of Anagni. Several Roman emperors were known to have used it, including Antoninus Pius and Marcus Aurelius. A monastery was built on the ruins of the villa in the 6th century, but today it is also in ruins.

www.cattedraledianagni.it
www.archeoares.it/en/palazzo-bonifacio-anagni/

Garden of Ninfa

Ninfa was an ancient village that derived its name from a *nympheum*, or a temple dedicated to water nymphs. In the Roman era, the town was the center of a small farming community, which progressively grew wealthier because of its proximity to the Appian Way. The town likely hit its peak with the inauguration of Pope Alexander III in Ninfa's Church of Santa Maria Maggiore in 1159. Unfortunately, the village was destroyed by troops loyal to an antipope (i.e., a rebel pope who doesn't recognize the actual pope) in 1382, during the Great Schism (definitely look that one up). And it was never rebuilt. For a time it was known as *La Città Morta di Ninfa*, or the Dead City of Ninfa.

Over the succeeding centuries, various members of the Caetani family, who came to own the village ruins, created gardens at Ninfa attempting to take advantage of abundant available water. But ubiquitous malaria, thanks to the mosquito-infested wetlands, posed a deadly problem. That changed in the early 20th century, however, when the Caetani family once

again created a garden in this unique landscape of historic ruins, which includes both a lake and a stream. Today, Ninfa is managed by the Roffredo Caetani Foundation and encompasses a 105-hectare park, including over 8 hectares of world-famous gardens.

Why go? The Garden of Ninfa is one of the most beautiful gardens in Europe and is known as the most romantic garden in the world. Planned generally in an overgrown English style, the juxtaposition of the medieval ruins with over 1,300 species of plants collected from around the world is stunning. It is almost impossible to take a bad photograph of the castle tower at the edge of the lake or the ancient stone bridge over the stream. The wetlands and vegetation of Ninfa also attract over 150 bird species, many of which migrate between Europe and Africa.

 Where? The Garden of Ninfa is 52 kilometers southeast of Rome and it will take over an hour to drive there. It is also possible to take a train from Rome-Termini to Latina and switch to a bus to the village of Norma. But that still puts you a couple kilometers away from the gardens, which you could either walk (over a very steep hill with many switchbacks) or, better yet, take a taxi.

 Cost and time? The garden is still in private ownership and entrance is by reservation only. It costs €15 for an adult, kids under 12 are FREE, and it takes about an hour to see it.

 Kids? The Garden of Ninfa is a great place for all kids. Though it is not a public park, everyone can appreciate a walk through ancient ruins surrounded by lush green vegetation and flowing streams.

 Guide? Entry into the garden is allowed only with a guide from the foundation, who is usually well versed in botany.

 When? The garden is generally open from the end of March to the beginning of November. It can be visited in the off-season by

reservation as well, but for a more expensive flat rate. Booked
tours happen in the rain or the sunshine, so watch the forecast.

FUN FACTS

* The Garden of Ninfa was one of the inspirations for the novel *The
  Garden of the Finzi-Continis* (1962) by Giorgio Bassani and the resulting
  Oscar-winning movie (1971).
* The World Wildlife Fund recognizes the importance of the habitats that
  the Garden of Ninfa provides to migratory bird species.

*Enrichment: In the summer, there are weekly jazz concerts at Ninfa for
an additional fee. The Caetani Foundation also manages the 13th-century
Caetani Castle in Sermoneta, only 4 kilometers southeast of the garden
(only open to the public in the summer). The Valvisciolo Cistercian Abbey
is also less than 3 kilometers from Ninfa. The ruins of Norba, another dead
city dating back to at least 500 BC, are only a kilometer northeast of Ninfa.
Norba may not have brilliant gardens, but it has great panoramic views
and it's FREE.*

www.frcaetani.it/en/garden-of-ninfa

www.52jazz.com

Palace of the Popes in Viterbo

In the 12th and 13th centuries, a power struggle was developing between the
Catholic Church in Rome and the Holy Roman Empire, a growing force ema-
nating from central Europe. Both were attempting to be the primary voice
of Christianity. When forces loyal to the empire in Rome, called Ghibellines,
become powerful enough to force Pope Alexander IV into exile in 1257, he

© Ufficio Comunicazione Polo Monumentale Colle del Duomo

moved to the city of Viterbo, north of Rome, and established the *Palazzo dei Papi*. Over the next 24 years, eight popes lived mostly in Viterbo. But when Pope Martin IV, a Frenchman, was elected in 1281, he moved the roaming papacy to Orvieto, thanks to the long history of French-Italian competition. Today, the Palace of the Popes in Viterbo is a testament to all these medieval shenanigans and can be toured along with the associated Cathedral of San Lorenzo and the Museum of the Cathedral Hill.

Why go? The 13th-century palace is still the primary symbol of the city of Viterbo. The architecture, including the bell tower and *Piazza San Lorenzo*, is beautiful and worth the trip alone. The museums contain exhibits on the popes and the church, of course, but also highlight the Etruscan society that predated the Romans.

 Where? The city of Viterbo is 66 kilometers north-northwest of central Rome. It takes about an hour and a half to drive there, but a direct train goes from Rome-Termini to Viterbo about 15 times per day. The cost is roughly €10 one way and takes about two hours.

 Cost and time? The entrance fee for all three of papal attractions together is €9 for an adult. A visit to the papal complex should take a couple of hours.

 Kids? Teens may appreciate the history associated with the papal palace, but younger kids may wonder why "we came all the way here to see another church?" The medieval alleyways of old Viterbo, however, may yield a gelato shop or two. There are also some good photo opportunities for kids interested in photography.

Guide? The entrance fee includes an audio guide.

When? Viterbo is a classic road trip destination from Rome. September 3rd is the annual *Macchina di Santa Rosa* procession, when 100 strong people dressed all in white (with red sashes) carry a 28-meter tower of light through the streets and alleys of the old town. There are also a lot of adventures in this part of Lazio so it's easy to combine visiting the papal palace with other destinations.

FUN FACTS

* Opposed to the Ghibellines, the faction that supported the pope during the Middle Ages was called the Guelphs.
* The first cardinal conclave to select a pope happened in Viterbo in 1268. It took three years to select Pope Gregory X in 1271!
* Pope John XXI died in Viterbo when parts of the Papal Palace roof caved in on him in 1277.

Enrichment: *Many TV shows and movies, including parts of* La Dolce Vita *(1960),* Life Is Beautiful *(1997), and* The Godfather: Part III *(1990), were filmed in the* comune *(or municipality) of Viterbo because of the unique architecture found there. Other adventures in this book within 20 kilometers of city of Viterbo include the monster sculptures of* Sacro Bosco *in* Bomarzo, *Lago di Vico, the Baths of Viterbo, the Church of San Pietro in Tuscania, and the* Palazzo Farnese *in Caprarola.*

≡ www.archeoares.it/en/palazzo-dei-papi-3/

The Renaissance

Palazzo Farnese of Rome

Palazzo Farnese is a beautiful 16th century palace built by the influential Farnese family adjacent to the Tiber River in central Rome. Initially commissioned by Alessandro Farnese, who later became Pope Paul III, it is the product of many well-known architects and artists, including Michelangelo. The Farnese family eventually married into the House of Bourbon and moved much of their accumulated paintings and sculptures to their palace in Naples, but that did not dim the beauty of this palace. *Palazzo Farnese* has been the French Embassy since 1874.

Why go? This is perhaps the best representation of a Renaissance palace in Rome. Inside are opulent galleries and ballrooms covered in amazing frescoes and crowned with stunning ceilings. The gardens on the backside of *Palazzo Farnese* originally went down to the Tiber River. They have been abbreviated over the years but remain a green urban oasis.

 Where? *Palazzo Farnese* is about a kilometer west of *Piazza Venezia* and only 100 meters south of *Campo de' Fiori*. It's a 15-minute walk from *Piazza Venezia* to *Palazzo Farnese*, or there are several bus routes (46, 62, 64, 916) that can get you closer.

 Cost and time? Admission to the palace is only through designated tours by the French Embassy that must be reserved at least a week ahead of time. Sometimes the wait for space on a tour can be months. Check their website for details.

 Kids? Kids have to be at least 10 years old to be allowed into the Embassy, but if they can get in, the tour is short and the palace is so cool!

 Guide? Visitors are only allowed into the Embassy on a guided tour.

 When? The best time to go to *Palazzo Farnese* is anytime that you can get a tour reservation.

FUN FACTS

＊ The primary architect of Palazzo Farnese, Antonio da Sangallo the Younger, also built parts of the Vatican and Saint Patrick's Well in Orvieto.

＊ The palace was purchased by the French Government in 1911 and sold back to the Italian Government, who then leased it back to the French for a reported €1 per year.

Enrichment: Palazzo Farnese *in Rome is not to be confused with* Palazzo Farnese *in Caprarola, also an adventure in this book. The Farnese family developed a sort of capital for their dynasty in the city of Castro (west of Lake Bolsena and the present-day village of Farnese), which was later razed in 1649 when the family fell out of favor with Pope Innocent X. Today, it is possible to hike into the ruins through a regrown forest. The Farnese art collection is currently in the Naples National Archeological Museum* (Museo Archeologico Nazionale di Napoli *[MANN]*)*.

≡ www.it.ambafrance.org/Visiter-le-Palais-Farnese-414
≡ www.mannapoli.it

Villa Borghese

Villa Borghese is the most amazing city park in Rome (and maybe the world), sitting at the edge of the central district above *Piazza del Popolo* and atop the Spanish Steps. Originally developed from vineyards into gardens by Cardinal Borghese (nephew of Pope Paul V) at the beginning of the 17th century, the 80-hectare park now features almost everything you might want in an urban recreation area. Not only does it have pleasant walking trails under a canopy of beautiful trees and an awesome overlook of the city, it has museums (including *Galleria Borghese*, *Museo Pietro Canonica*, and *Museo Carlo Bilotti*), theaters (The Globe, *Cinema dei Piccoli*, and San Carlino Puppet Theater), restaurants, a dog park, an exercise track, an outdoor cinema, and an equestrian center. The *Bioparco di Roma* (Rome's zoo) takes up one corner of *Villa Borghese*, and you can rent rowboats on a small lake beside a non-ancient temple. There are also 4-wheel bike rentals and a mini tourist train to help you get around.

Why go? The overlook above *Piazza del Popolo*, called the Pincio Terrace, is reason enough to visit *Villa Borghese*, let alone all the other things listed above. Even in the rain, *Villa Borghese* is a fun place to be.

Where? The park is less than 1.5 kilometers north from *Piazza Venezia* through Centro Storico. The Spagna subway stop (Line A) is near the Spanish Steps and the Flaminio stop (also Line A) is near *Piazza del Popolo*. The park is a short walk from either stop, though uphill. Many city bus routes go through or near the park.

Cost and time? The park itself is FREE, but the attractions in the park may cost money. *Galleria Borghese* also requires reservations. You can never spend too much time in *Villa Borghese*.

Kids? Of course! There are also two playgrounds in the park and a small carousel.

 Guide? Though guides may be useful in some of the museums, and indeed compulsory in *Villa Medici*, in the park itself all you really need is a map. If you are short on time, however, there are bicycle tours of the park that cover a lot of ground.

 When? Anytime, though maybe not after dark. Sunset on the Pincio Terrace is a must!

FUN FACTS

* Often there are temporary outdoor art installations throughout *Villa Borghese*.
* There is a hydroclock in the park that was built in 1867 and is still powered by running water.
* Near the overlook are 228 busts of prestigious Italian personalities. The bust of Angelo Secchi, a 19th century astronomer, includes a

hole through its base that sights the Rome Meridian, which was only supplanted as the basis for mapping Italy by the Greenwich Meridian in 1964.

~~~~~~

Enrichment: *With all the things to do in* Villa Borghese, *there is also so much to see just around its edges. There are the gardens of* Villa Medici, *the Etruscan artifacts at* Villa Giulia, *and the paintings and sculpture at the National Gallery of Modern and Contemporary Art. There is* Piazza del Popolo *and the Caravaggio paintings in the adjacent basilica.*

☰ www.galleriaborghese.beniculturali.it/en/visita/info-biglietti/

For more details, search for websites for individual features of Villa Borghese, of which there are many.

ADVENTURE #XXXI

Villa Medici

Villa Medici is a large 16th-century palace that sits between the top of the Spanish Steps and *Villa Borghese*. Originally commissioned by the family of Cardinal Giovanni Ricci in 1564, it was later acquired and completed by Cardinal Ferdinando de' Medici, the Grand Duke of Tuscany. When the Medici lineage of male heirs ended in 1737, the villa passed through various royal families, eventually ending up with Napoleon Bonaparte. In 1803, wanting to preserve its function as a place for selected French artists to study art and architecture, Napoleon moved the *French Academy in Rome* into the villa. Today, the Academy continues its prestigious arts fellowship program at *Villa Medici* by hosting 16 artists annually. In conjunction with the Academy, the villa hosts a series of temporary artistic exhibitions. Behind the villa building itself are over seven hectares of ornate gardens that are open to the public on guided tours.

Why go? There are usually only a few indoor rooms open on the tours of *Villa Medici*; the real attraction is the outdoor garden and the exterior bas-relief sculptures on the garden-side of the building. While the front of the villa is not particularly interesting other than its obvious size, the garden side is uniquely beautiful. There is a replica of an 8th century BC Egyptian obelisk in the garden, along with ancient Roman artifacts. The view of central Rome from the garden overlook rivals the view from any hilltop in the city.

 Where? *Villa Medici* is less than 1.5 kilometers north of *Piazza Venezia*. The Spagna subway stop on Line A is nearby, or climb to the top of the Spanish Steps and turn left. You can't miss it. Don't let the armed security out front put you off.

 Cost and time? Tours of the garden and art exhibit cost €14/adult and take about 90 minutes. Online reservations are recommended. Tours are in Italian, French, or English, so check their website before you go to catch the right one.

 Kids? The gardens are beautiful, but the tour of the garden does not allow for playtime.

 Guide? Admission to the garden is only via internal guided tour. The exhibit space is also only accessible on a tour.

 When? It's a relatively short tour, so go when you're planning to be in the neighborhood or combine a visit with another adventure. There is so much to do nearby!

FUN FACTS

* The *Villa Medici* sits on the ruins of an ancient Roman villa, though when it was conceived the land was mostly a vineyard.

✳ The powerful Medici family, originally from Tuscany, produced three popes and were the patrons of many Renaissance artists, including Leonardo da Vinci, Michelangelo, and Raphael.

✳ The idea of the French Academy in Rome may have originated from Bernini, who suggested in 1665 that young French artists could gain from the experience of spending some time in Rome. The fellows of the Academy are called *pensionnaires*.

Enrichment: *There is a café inside* Villa Medici, *which captures the aura of the villa and provides great views of the city. It is also possible to stay at* Villa Medici *when their lodging is not in use for other functions. Some of the Renaissance rooms are fantastic. It is predictably expensive, and reservations need to be made at least four months in advance.* Villa Medici *is literally just a stone's throw from* Villa Borghese, *with the Pincio Terrace,* Galleria Borghese, *zoo, and everything else the park has to offer.*

☰ www.villamedici.it

Palazzo Altemps

The *Palazzo Altemps* is a 15th century palace located just north of *Piazza Navona*. It was built by a pope's nephew, Girolamo Riario, who held a murderous grudge against the Medici family of Florence, and was himself eventually a victim of assassination. It was named after Cardinal Marco Altemps, who bought the palace in 1568. At the end of the 19th century, the Vatican bought the residence to use it as a seminary. In 1982, the palace became the property of the Italian government and was converted into a museum specializing in classic sculptures and temporary exhibits. The museum at *Palazzo Altemps* is one of four that encompass the National Museum of Rome (*Museo Nazionale Romano*).

Why go? Like other beautiful Renaissance palaces in Rome that have been converted to art museums, the *Palazzo Altemps* is an excellent example of stunning galleries exhibiting amazing sculptures. Entry to the museum is through an open-roofed courtyard with two stories of arches, some filled

with statues. Many of the pleasant exhibit rooms have frescoed walls and wooden ceilings, and display sculptures from several collections, including from the Altemps and Ludovisi families, and go back as far as the 5th century BC. Some of the previously damaged ancient statues were restored by famous sculptors, such as Bernini. The temporary exhibits, including paintings, change over time, but often provide a unique juxtaposition of modern and classic art. There are also a small church, theater, tower, and bookstore in the palace.

 Where? *Palazzo Altemps* is located about a kilometer northwest of *Piazza Venezia*. There is no nearby subway station, but it is only 50 meters north of *Piazza Navona*.

 Cost and time? At the time of publication, there was an online €12 ticket that allowed access to all the locations of the National Museum of Rome, including *Crypta Balbi*, *Palazzo Massimo*, and the Baths of Diocletian. The *Palazzo Altemps* museum will take a couple of hours to see.

 Kids? Not particularly.

 Guide? Like any good museum, there is a lot of interesting background information to every piece of art. The museum does a good job at describing each piece with an accompanying wall poster.

 When? This is a great museum to enjoy when the weather is not friendly for outdoor adventures.

FUN FACTS
* Given its location in the center of the city, *Palazzo Altemps* was also undoubtedly built on ruins from ancient Rome.
* The courtyard of the current palace sometimes hosts live music concerts.

✳ The Ludovisi family once had a grand 17th-century palace where the U.S. Embassy stands today that contained their extensive art collection. Facing crippling debt in 1885, the family sold the contents of the villa and the buildings were demolished to subdivide the land for redevelopment. The only remaining building from the original villa is the *Casino dell'Aurora*.

~~~~~~

Enrichment: *Other palaces turned art museums in Rome include* Palazzo Barberini, Palazzo Corsini, Palazzo Braschi, *and the Doria Pamphilj Gallery. There is so much to see in the area immediately around* Palazzo Altemps, *including* Piazza Navona, Castel Sant'Angelo, *the Ara Pacis Museum, and the Mausoleum of Augustus.*

☰ www.museonazionaleromano.beniculturali.it/en/palazzo-altemps/

ADVENTURE #XXXIII

The Jewish Quarter

Originally emigrating from Judea, the Jewish community has been a part of Rome since at least the 2nd century BC. By the middle of the 16th century AD, there were several thousand Jews in Rome. Also at that time, the Catholic Church had evolved toward a rigid orthodoxy and an authoritarian manner. Pope Paul IV decreed in 1555 that all Jews in Rome live in a 3-hectare ghetto, walled with three gates that were locked at night. Jews could leave during the day but had to wear yellow; kerchiefs for women and caps for men. The ghetto had narrow alleyways that flooded frequently due to the proximity to the Tiber River, and was prone to malaria and cholera. As the population grew inside the ghetto, peaking at about 10,000 people, living conditions worsened. With limited space, the only way to expand was to build additional floors on already tenuous foundations. Eventually, sunlight

seldom reached street level. The Papal States ceased to exist with Italian unification in 1870 (a.k.a. Risorgimento), and Jews were no longer required to live in the ghetto; however, the persecution did not end. During WWII, the occupying German forces in Italy sent 2,000 Jews, many from the former ghetto, to the concentration camps in Germany.

Today, the Jewish Quarter encompasses what is left of the ghetto. Most of the original shoddy buildings have been replaced, but it is still possible to get a glimpse of one of the ghetto gates and a few of the old buildings. Brass nameplates have been installed in the sidewalk identifying where those lost to the German purge once lived. Unlike many other European ghettos that are now tourist attractions or museums, the Jewish Quarter of Rome is still the active center of the Jewish community in Rome, with a synagogue, schools, restaurants, a bookstore, and an awesome bakery.

Why go? The Jewish Quarter is a monument to the horrendous conditions that the Jewish community has had to endure, not just in Rome or during WWII, but throughout Europe and for centuries.

Where? The Jewish Quarter is about 0.6 kilometers southwest of *Piazza Venezia*, adjacent to the Tiber River. The fastest way to get there is to walk.

 Cost and time? The quarter encompasses only a few streets and alleys, and will take only an hour or so to see. It is FREE to walk around the neighborhood.

 Kids? Though the history of Jewish people in Rome is a challenging topic, it is something everyone should know about. It may not me appropriate for younger kids.

 Guide? Yes, a guide will be very helpful in describing the conditions that once faced the Jewish people of Rome.

 When? Anytime.

FUN FACTS

* Italy is currently home to about 43,000 Jews.
* The restaurants in the neighborhood are known for their deep-fried artichokes, among other traditional dishes.
* A small hourglass-shaped remembrance was created by Israeli artist Micha Ullman in *Piazza di Monte Savello*, near the Jewish Quarter, to commemorate the coexistence of two cultures.

Enrichment: In 1904, the Great Synagogue of Rome was built between the historic Jewish Quarter and the Tiber River. There is a Jewish museum inside the synagogue, which also runs 45-minute tours of the neighborhood (€8/adult).

www.romaebraica.it
www.museoebraico.roma.it/en/

Capuchin Crypt

The Capuchin Crypt (*Cripta dei Cappuccini*) is decorated with the bones of 3,700 Capuchin friars that died between 1528 and 1870. The Capuchins are an order of the Catholic Church that believes in austerity, simplicity, and poverty. The crypt consists of six small rooms under the Church of Our Lady of the Conception of the Capuchin (*Santa Maria della Concezione dei Cappuccini*). The bones are arranged into various structures including separate rooms for leg bones, pelvises, and skulls. There is a small museum about the Capuchins before entering the crypt, which also has a painting purportedly by Caravaggio.

Why go? Though the intended message of the crypt is to highlight the fleeting nature of life ("What you are now we used to be; what we are now you will be"), the place is still pretty creepy. In the museum there is a catalogue of the friars whose bones are in the crypt, which is the primary reminder that the bones were once real people instead of sculptural props.

 Where? The Capuchin Crypt is about a kilometer northwest of *Piazza Venezia*, and adjacent to *Piazza Barberini*. The Barberini subway stop on the A Line is less than 100 meters away, and not far from *Palazzo Barberini*.

 Cost and time? The entrance fee for the crypt is €8.50/adult. It will take about an hour to go through the museum and the crypt. They also rent shawls if you are not dressed appropriately (it's a holy place).

 Kids? Teens and tweens might love the creepiness of the place, but younger kids probably won't.

 Guide? The museum gives tours in English for an extra €80 for a group (make reservation in advance). They also rent audio guides for €5.

 When? Since it's inside, a good time to go to the crypt is during bad weather or during the heat of the day. The best time of year would be around Halloween, All Souls' Day, or *Dia de los Muertos*.

FUN FACTS

* Capuchin friars dress in a plain brown tunic with a hood, fastened around the waist. They typically have beards and wear sandals.
* Your morning cappuccino is so named because it shares the color of the friars' tunics.
* When friars died during the lifetime of the crypt, they were buried in soil for thirty years to decompose before their bones were moved to the crypt.

Enrichment: *If creepy is what you're after, check out the Museum of the Holy Souls in Purgatory at the back of* Chiesa del Sacro Cuore del Suffragio, *not far from* Castel Sant'Angelo.

≡ www.cappucciniviaveneto.it/#english

ADVENTURE #XXXV

Villa d'Este in Tivoli

Villa d'Este is a classically beautiful, though unfinished, Renaissance villa in the hill town of Tivoli. It was built by Cardinal Ippolito d'Este in the 16th century and is most known for its amazing garden on a terraced hillside, filled with fountains. The waterworks were the first of their kind in Europe and were soon copied elsewhere. The villa itself is equally as impressive, with beautiful frescoes and stunning views of the surrounding landscape. It is a UNESCO World Heritage Site.

Why go? This is one of the "must visit" villas. Almost every room of the villa has incredibly ornate ceilings and the garden exudes a mystical aura somewhere between controlled and mature verdant chaos. The Oval Fountain (*Fontana dell'Ovato*) and the Hundred Fountains (*Cento Fontane*) are particularly spectacular.

 Where? The Tivoli train station is 28 kilometers east-northeast from central Rome. A train leaves Rome-Termini for Tivoli almost every hour (starting at €3). A bus regularly goes from the Tivoli train station to *Villa d'Este* for €1.30. It also takes less than an hour to drive there.

 Cost and time? The fee to get into *Villa d'Este* is €12/adult. There is a lot to see in the villa and gardens so it will take at least two or three hours.

 Kids? The fountains in the *Villa d'Este* garden are pretty fantastic, no matter how old you are. And teenagers will love to see what it was like to live in a villa with enormous wealth 500 years ago.

 Guide? Absolutely, *Villa d'Este* is so large and beautiful that you will learn so much more about it with a tour guide.

 When? Nice days. One of the reasons Cardinal d'Este escaped Rome for the city of Tivoli was because the summertime at altitude is marginally cooler. That said, it can still get quite warm in Tivoli in August, though the fountains in the *Villa d'Este* do have a cooling effect.

✳ Unfortunately, Cardinal d'Este pilfered building material for his dream home from Hadrian's Villa in the valley below, causing the latter to lose some of its luster.

✳ Water from the nearby Aniene River is diverted to feed the fountains.

✳ The famous water organ in the garden wasn't functional for over two centuries until reconstruction was completed in 2003. The organ plays several times per day, but check at the villa entrance for playing times before heading in.

✳ The center of the d'Este family empire is in the city of Ferrara in present-day Emilia-Romagna.

Enrichment: *Other sites in the town of Tivoli include the park* Villa Gregoriana *with trails and waterfalls, the remains of a 2nd century AD amphitheater* (Anfiteatro di Bleso)*, the Sanctuary of Hercules Victor, and* Rocca Pia*, a medieval fortress. Hadrian's Villa, an ancient country estate fit for an emperor, is only 3 kilometers from* Villa d'Este.

www.levillae.com/en/

www.villadestetivoli.info/indexe.htm

www.visittivoli.eu/archeologia/santuario-di-ercole-vincitore&lang=EN

ADVENTURE #XXXVI

Palazzo Farnese of Caprarola

Palazzo Farnese is a fortress that sits above the town of Caprarola, in addition to the name of a palace in Rome. It was built in the 16th century by the wealthy Farnese family and is famed for its pentagonal shape, its inner circular courtyard, and its ornate spiral staircase. Coming from town, the entrance to the palace is a little daunting, with an uphill climb to the front door. But once inside, the frescoed walls and ceilings of the galleries and stairway are amazing, particularly in the map room, which depicts the understanding of the world in the late 1500s.

Why go? *Palazzo Farnese* is another awesome display of the wealth and power of the Farnese family. Architecturally, it is unique and beautiful, and the grounds are one of the best examples of a Renaissance garden.

 Where? Caprarola is 52 kilometers from Rome to the north-northwest. The easiest way to get there is by car and takes a little over an hour. There isn't a train station in town, but it is possible to get there from Rome via a series of buses.

 Cost and time? The entrance fee for *Palazzo Farnese* is €5/ person. Walking through the palace and gardens will take a couple of hours.

 Kids? Teens and tweens will love to see the country house of the super-rich circa 1550. It might be harder to keep littler kids engaged, but you could give them a camera and a photographic mission to keep them focused longer (e.g., take a picture of the all the birds that you see).

 Guide? Yes, hearing stories about horses climbing the stairs can bring the villa to life.

 When? Closed on Mondays. Go in the spring or summer, when the gardens are at their best.

FUN FACTS

✴ An American woman, Florence Baldwin, and her three daughters lived in the palace from 1896 to 1918. Ms. Baldwin had fled from France after her husband killed her French boyfriend, and more than 20 years later

she was found dead at the base of one of the *Palazzo Farnese* stairways, or so the story goes.

∗ Currently, the palace's casino, or garden pavilion, serves as a country house for Italy's president.

∗ *Palazzo Farnese* of Caprarola is not to be confused with *Palazzo Farnese* or *Villa Farnesina* in Rome, which are two other adventures in this book.

Enrichment: *There are many other interesting adventures in this book that are nearby to Caprarola, including the monsters of Bomarzo,* Villa Lante, *the papal palace in Viterbo,* Lago di Vico, *and the artists' colony at Calcata. Visit several of the adventures and make a weekend out of it.*

☰ www.polomusealelazio.beniculturali.it/index.php?it/239/palazzo-farnese

Castello di Bracciano

Castello di Bracciano is a 15th century castle that sits on a hill overlooking *Lago di Bracciano*. Also known as *Castello Orsini-Odescalchi*, the castle was originally built by the Orsini family around a medieval fortress that dates back to the 13th century. The Orsinis produced three popes and married into the Medici family. In 1696, the castle was bought by the Odescalchi family, and they still own it today. *Castello di Bracciano* has been open to the public as a museum since 1952, and you can now rent it as your wedding venue.

Why go? *Castello di Bracciano* is one of the best-preserved Renaissance castles in Italy. There are several layers of fortifications around the castle, including classic turrets at the corners of the high walls. As picturesque as the outside is, it is equally beautiful inside, with a wide staircase leading to a courtyard lined with two stories of medieval arches. The rooms still have period furniture, paintings, frescoes, and wooden ceilings — there is even a room of ancient weaponry. The view of Lake Bracciano out the castle windows is stupendous.

Where? The town of Bracciano is 35 kilometers northwest of central Rome. It takes an hour to drive there. Trains leave Rome-Tiburtina about 20 times a day for Bracciano, and stop at other Rome train stations along the way. It takes 90 minutes and costs roughly €5 one way.

 Cost and time? The cost to get into *Castello di Bracciano* is €8.50/adult. You could easily spend an hour wandering around.

 Kids? Yes, the castle has special activities for kids including a visit with a princess (one hour, €6/kid ages 3+ and €8.50/adult), and a castle escape (two hours, €15/person for ages five and up). Check the website for details.

 Guide? The castle offers various kinds of tours for adults including a basic private tour (one hour, €120 for 10 people), a cocktail tour (two hours, €300 for 12 people), and an adventure tour (three hours, €29/person), which includes climbing the walls and rappelling into a cistern!

 When? Might as well make a summer day of it with a morning visit to the castle and an afternoon at the beach on Lake Bracciano. Partway around the lake is the medieval village of Anguillara Sabazia, which has a lakefront promenade that is perfect for a sunset *aperitivo*.

~~~~~~

FUN FACTS

* Pope Sixtus IV stayed in the castle in 1481 to escape the plague that was infesting Rome.
* If this castle sounds right out of a movie, it is. Many films and television shows have been staged here including *Bill and Ted's Excellent Adventure* (1989).

* Many well-known people have used the castle for their wedding reception, including Martin Scorsese/Isabella Rossellini and Tom Cruise/ Katie Holmes.
* Technically, the castle is on the rim of a volcanic crater.

Enrichment: *The small village of Bracciano is worth exploring. The beach community of Lake Bracciano is just down the hill from the village and includes beach clubs and windsurfing/sailing schools. When you are windsurfing, be sure look up at the castle every once in a while. It will take your breath away!*

≡ www.odescalchi.it

ADVENTURE #XXXVIII

Villa Lante in Bagnaia

There are two nearly identical, square, late-Renaissance houses (*casini*) at *Villa Lante*, each built in the late 16th century. The first one was constructed by Cardinal Gambara in 1566, and the second was built by a teenaged Cardinal Montalto nearly 30 years later. The primary difference between them is the style of the frescoes painted inside. But the true star of this villa is the garden, which features waterfalls, fountains, and other water features over five levels of terraces. Modeled somewhat on the gardens of *Villa d'Este* in Tivoli, which were built around the same time, the gardens and park at *Villa Lante* cover nearly 16 hectares. The villa's name comes from Duke Ippolito Lante, who acquired the villa in 1656. Restored after WWII, the gardens are now administered by the regional government and are open to the public.

Why go? The gardens of *Villa Lante* are both in front of the *casini*, where they greet arriving visitors, and extensively at the back, where they are

tiered with increasing elevation. There are stairs between terraces with water running down the middle, a long stone table with a middle channel of cooling water, dripping nymph caves, and a pavilion at the top/back of the garden. Access to the inside of the *casini* is often limited, but they are worthy of a visit when open.

 Where? The town of Bagnaia is 65 kilometers north-northwest of Rome, and 4 kilometers east of Viterbo. It takes about an hour and 15 minutes to drive from central Rome. There is also a train from Rome, but it requires switching trains in Viterbo. That trip could take two and half to three hours.

 Cost and time? Entrance into *Villa Lante* is only €5/adult. To see the gardens and the buildings will take a couple of hours.

 Kids? Families with strollers will have a difficult time accessing the various terraces because of the steps, but kids will like the mesmerizing water features.

Guide? Appreciating the gardens on your own is easy, but a local guide could tell you stories of the history of the place.

 When? The best time to see the gardens of *Villa Lante* is in the late spring or early summer when the plants are green and the dry heat of the summer has yet to have an impact. The water features, however, help keep the garden cool even in the heat of the summer.

FUN FACTS

* The design and construction of the water features in the gardens must have required the very best, state-of-the-art architects and water engineers at that time for the water to still be flowing almost 500 years later.
* *Villa Lante* has been the setting for many movies and TV shows, including *The Young Pope* (2016).

Enrichment: *A visit to* Villa d'Este *and the Garden of Ninfa will help complete a tour of the water-oriented gardens in Lazio. Other adventures near* Villa Lante *include the Papal Palace in Viterbo,* Sacro Bosco *in Bomarzo, and Calcata.*

≡ www.polomusealelazio.beniculturali.it/index.php?it/243/villa-lante

Sacro Bosco in Bomarzo

Sacro Bosco, or the Sacred Grove, is also known as the Garden of Bomarzo and as the Park of the Monsters. Whatever the name, it is a magical garden filled with fantastical sculptures, created in the 16th century by Pier Francesco Orsini to cope with grief following the death of his wife. The garden had fallen into disrepair until championed by Salvador Dali in the 1950s and has since been restored into a private tourist attraction.

Why go? Large surreal sculptures along a forested walk . . . what's not to like?

 Where? *Sacro Bosco* is outside the village of Bomarzo and 70 kilometers north-northwest of central Rome. The best way to get

there is by car, and it will take about 90 minutes. It is possible to take a train from Rome to Attigliano-Bomarzo (€6), and then a taxi for the remaining 8 kilometers.

Cost and time? The park is not actually that big (it takes at most a couple of hours). The adult entrance fee to the park is €11. There is a small snack bar and souvenir shop on site.

Kids? The *Sacro Bosco* is a popular family attraction. Toddlers and little kids might be challenged by the walk, but they'll love the giant turtle.

Guide? It may not be necessary, but a guide will be able to tell you the story behind some of the bizarre attractions. Antonio Rocca has published an insightful guide to the sculptures, though it is currently available only in Italian.

When? Summertime is the best time to go, or anytime the weather is nice.

FUN FACTS

* All the sculptures were created from rocks found where they currently sit, including river rocks in the stream.
* This park might include the world's oldest fun house (i.e., it intentionally does not stand straight up).

Enrichment: Since the sculpture garden won't take you all day, why not combine it with a swim in nearby Lago di Vico *on the way back to Rome? Or the hot springs in Viterbo? If you are interested in eclectic outdoor sculpture, definitely check out* Il Giardino dei Tarocchi *(#LXII).*

☰ www.sacrobosco.it

Enlightenment, Unification, and Mussolini

Quartiere Coppedè

The *Quartiere Coppedè* (Coppedè District) is a neighborhood in north-east Rome that features buildings created in the unique *Art Nouveau* style of architect Gino Coppedè. Centered around the *Fontana delle Rane* (Fountain of Frogs) in *Piazza Mincio*, the district encompasses only a few square blocks with 35 buildings built between 1917 and shortly after Coppedè's death in 1927. Part of the project, once called the "Palaces of the Ambassadors", is still home to the embassies for South Africa, Morocco, and Bolivia.

Why go? The architecture of the buildings in this district is truly unique and different from anything found in Rome, or anywhere in the world for that matter. The detail is astounding with a whimsical quality to it, such as in the aptly named *Villino delle Fate* (Fairy Cottages). The icons of the neighborhood are the fountain, which has recently been restored, and the outdoor chandelier under Coppedè's arch, a two-story bridge between buildings and over the diagonal entranceway to the district over *Via Dora*.

 Where? *Quartiere Coppedè* is 3 kilometers northeast of *Piazza Venezia*. The closest subway stop is Policlinico on the B Line, then walk half a kilometer northwest or it's three stops on the 3 or 19 trams to *Piazza Buenos Aires*, also known to locals as *Piazza Quadrata*. The arch is one block northeast of the piazza. The 63, 83, and 92 buses also pass by the district from Rome-Termini Station and Centro.

 Cost and time? Walking around the Coppedè neighborhood is FREE. It's pretty small so it won't take much time. The interiors of the buildings are also supposed to be artistically unique, but they are typically closed to public access.

Kids? Kids probably won't be too excited about the architecture, but it makes a great stop on the way to the parks in the area, like *Villa Borghese*, *Ada*, and *Torlonia*.

 Guide? Probably. There is a lot of subtle detail to the architecture that might be more easily noticed and explained with a guide. How the neighborhood was planned and funded is also an interesting story.

 When? Anytime is good time for visiting this neighborhood. At night you can see the lit chandlier.

FUN FACTS

* There aren't any restaurants or stores in *Quartiere Coppedè*, though the surrounding neighborhoods have typical commercial streets.
* The Beatles were rumored to have taken a dip in the *Fontana delle Rane* after a late-night visit to the nearby Piper Club.
* Hundreds of movies have been filmed in *Quartiere Coppedè*, including *House of Gucci* (2021).

Enrichment: *Since the district is quite small, it makes sense to stop here on the way to other nearby adventures. For more whimsical architecture, check out the* Casina delle Civette *(House of the Little Owls) in* Villa Torlonia. *There are many parks (including* Parco Virgiliano*) and interesting catacombs (Priscilla and St. Agnes) within walking distance of the Coppedè District.*

Currently, there is no official website for the neighborhood.

Villa Torlonia

Villa Torlonia is a 13-hectare city park in a northeastern neighborhood of Rome. During the Renaissance, the area was primarily vineyards and orchards belonging to several prominent Roman families. The land was developed as an estate by three generations of the Torlonia family from the beginning of the 19th century. The villa was rented to Benito Mussolini in 1925 and he lived there until his arrest in 1943. The City of Rome acquired the land in 1977, at which point it was opened to the public as a park.

Why go? The park of *Villa Torlonia* is not just a place for people from the neighborhood to walk their dogs, exercise, and picnic with their friends. It is also a museum, a theater, a café, a bunker, and a catacomb. The primary palace, with a fantastic ballroom, and the *Casina delle Civette* (House of the Little Owls) have both been turned into a museum, which includes some of the artwork accumulated by the Torlonia family, a collection of stained

glass, and Mussolini's bedroom. *Teatro Torlonia* reopened in 2013 and is home to eclectic shows and performances. *La Limonaia* is a café in the villa's greenhouse and has both indoor and outdoor dining. Tours are usually available of Mussolini's airtight bunker under the villa, but the Jewish catacombs, from the 3rd century and only rediscovered in 1919, are not yet open to the public.

 Where? *Villa Torlonia* is about 3 kilometers northeast of *Piazza Venezia*. The closest subway stop is Policlinico on the B Line, and then a two-block walk north. Many bus lines from Centro and Rome-Termini go down *Via Nomentana*, which fronts the villa.

 Cost and time? Entrance into the park is FREE but getting into the museum is €11/person. A tour of the bunker is €10/person and reservations must be made in advance. Depending on your interest, it could take half a day to see the sites of Torlonia, or you could stroll through in 30 minutes and enjoy a granita at *La Limonaia*.

The museums at *Villa Torlonia* are part of Rome's vast system of 19 civic museums and 25 archeological sites. Residents of Rome qualify for a *Musei In Comune* (MIC) card that gets them into all of these museums for only €5 per year.

 Kids? Yes, *Villa Torlonia* is an outdoor park with lots of fun things to do. The kids may enjoy the eccentric architecture of the *Casina delle Civette* and there is a playground in *Villa Paganini*, the smaller park across *Via Nomentana*.

 Guide? Entrance is granted to the bunker only with a guided tour. Audio guides can be rented in the museum for €4.

 When? There are both indoor and outdoor things to do at *Villa Torlonia*, so any day is a good time to go. The outdoor café is particularly fun on a nice day.

FUN FACTS

∗ The Torlonia family built a fake Etruscan tomb in the basement of their villa. They also collected hundreds of marble statues, which will hopefully be displayed in their own museum sometime in the future.

∗ Prince Alessandro Torlonia, who built the somewhat eccentric *Casina delle Civette*, commemorated his parents by erecting two Egyptian-style obelisks at the villa in 1842. The stone for the monuments was quarried in Piedmont and traveled, primarily by boat (via lake, canal, rivers, and seas), 2,880 kilometers to Rome. For the last 4 kilometers, from the Aniene River to the villa, the boat was dragged overland. Each obelisk is just over 10 meters long and weighs about 22 tons. The whole city, including the pope, turned out for the dedication party, which included musical bands and fireworks.

Enrichment: *Nearby* Villa Albani *is of similar spatial scale to* Villa Torlonia *and is still in private ownership. It is sometimes open to the public under special arrangement. The gelato shop across* Via Nomentana *from the main entrance of* Villa Torlonia *puts liquid chocolate in the cone before putting your ice cream on top!*

www.museivillatorlonia.it/en

www.teatrodiroma.net/doc/5190/teatro-torlonia

www.limonaiaroma.it

www.bunkertorlonia.it

www.visitjewishitaly.it/en/listing/catacombs-of-villa-torlonia/

Villa Ada

Villa Ada is the second-largest (180 hectares) city park in Rome. Unlike *Villa Borghese*, which was planned and developed as a garden over its entire area, *Villa Ada* includes large swaths that are lightly managed (i.e., mostly forested). Named after the wife of a Swiss Count, the villa belonged to the Italian royal family (the House of Savoy) until 1946. Today, the Savoy Castle is the Egyptian embassy and the extensive park grounds are open to the public. There are walking paths to all sections of the park, a series of ponds (look for the turtles), rolling hills, and several cafés with outdoor terraces. Many Romans regularly use *Villa Ada* for recreation: meeting friends, walking dogs, and exercising. There is a private equestrian center in the middle of the park, and seeing mounted police out on patrol is common. There are also bicycles for rent near the big lake.

Why go? *Villa Ada* provides a small natural oasis in an otherwise urban landscape. Though many of the iconic umbrella pines are in decline, there are pockets of large trees among grassy meadows dotted with benches and picnickers. The royal family also had their own WWII bunker, which is usually open to the public for tours (by arrangement).

 Where? The park is 3.6 kilometers north-northeast of *Piazza Venezia*. The closest subway stop is Sant'Agnese-Annibaliano on the B Line, but it is still about a kilometer southeast of the park. Many city bus lines (63, 83, 92, 168) can get you closer. *Via Salaria* is the primary road outside the villa walls that heads toward the city center.

 Cost and time? Access to *Villa Ada* is FREE. It is easy to spend half a day exploring the park.

 Kids? Yes, the park is great for kids. There is a playground adjacent to one of the ponds and two areas that offer small amusement rides for children.

Guide? Though the park itself is fine without a guide, there are guided tours of the royal bomb shelter (check online for current details). There are also more extensive guided tours of the Savoy family history, which take in several sites in Rome including *Palazzo del Quirinale*, currently the official residence of the President of Italy.

When? Good weather days!

~~~~~~

FUN FACTS

✳ Mussolini was dismissed as the Italian Prime Minister and arrested by King Victor Emmanuel III at the Savoy Castle in *Villa Ada* in 1943. He was held at an isolated alpine prison at *Campo Imperatore* in the Abruzzo Region until German commandos successfully carried out a daring rescue and took him to Germany.

✳ Look for the green parrots nesting in the trees of *Villa Ada*. They are rose-ringed parakeets, not native to Rome.

~~~~~~

Enrichment: In the summertime, the island in the largest lake of Villa Ada *hosts live music shows every night, ranging from Italian pop to international blues. Though most of the shows require tickets to be in front of the stage (the cost depends on the act), a temporary village is constructed backstage where there is FREE access to food and drink from a variety of vendors and you can hear the music wafting in the wind. Even if you've never heard of the band, it can still be a fun evening's activity.*

www.villaada.org

www.bunkervillaada.it

EUR

The *Esposizione Universale Roma* (EUR) is a planned neighborhood in south Rome that was initiated by Benito Mussolini in 1936 to celebrate 20 years of fascism and the 1942 World's Fair/Exposition. The plans called for large stone buildings, in a style later to be known as fascist architecture, along wide boulevards. The exhibition never happened, however, because of WWII. Following the war, the Italian Government continued the project as an economic engine to create both needed construction jobs and a modern business district. It was almost fully completed by the time Rome hosted the 1960 Summer Olympics. Today, the buildings still look immense and the streets broad, which creates a distinctly different feel from the rest of Rome.

Why go? The grand systematic plan of EUR has very nearly been realized, but it lacks the soul and spirit of the rest of Rome. Built somewhat symmetrically around *Via Cristoforo Colombo*, the architectural icons of the neighborhood are impressive: the *Palazzo della Civiltà Italiana* (a.k.a. The Fendi Building or The Square Colosseum), the *Palazzo dei Congressi*, the Basilica of Saints Peter and Paul, the Marconi Obelisk (which is really a stelae), and the other oppressively bureaucratic-looking buildings. At the south end of EUR is *Laghetto dell'EUR* (or EUR Pond), which is a large artificial lake with beautiful waterfalls, and Palasport, the primary indoor sports arena for the city. More recently, *La Nuvola* (The Cloud) Conference Center, designed by Massimiliano Fuksas, added some modern architectural flair to the district along *Via Cristoforo Colombo*.

 Where? The EUR quarter is 7 kilometers south of *Piazza Venezia* and is served by three subways stations on the B Line: EUR Magliana, EUR Palasport, and EUR Fermi.

 Cost and time? Walking the neighborhood and seeing the architecture is, of course, FREE.

 Kids? Luneur Park, a small amusement park targeting smaller kids, is on the north edge of EUR.

 Guide? Absolutely! There are a lot of stories and architectural detail associated with EUR, including sculptures, mosaics, and frescoes, that a guide can bring to life. Can you find the bas-relief of Mussolini on a horse?

 When? A walking tour of EUR is best done on a nice weather day.

FUN FACTS

✳ *Laghetto dell'EUR* has hosted dragon boat races, water polo tournaments, and a floating summer cinema. The cherry trees around the lake explode with blossoms in the springtime.

✳ Combining two contemporary Roman icons, the Fendi fashion company made the Square Colosseum their headquarters in 2015.

✳ There are many museums in EUR, including the *Museo delle Civilt*à (Museum of Civilizations) and the *Museo della Civilt*à *Romana* (Museum of Roman Civilization), which was closed in 2014 for renovation and has yet to reopen.

✳ A commercial aquarium is currently being planned in the neighborhood.

Enrichment: *Other large construction projects during the Mussolini era include the* Foro Italico, *a sports complex built to host the 1940 Olympics, which were ultimately cancelled, and* Città Universitaria di Roma, *home to* La Sapienza, *one of the oldest and largest universities in Europe. Both projects eventually proved to be very successful. If you go to* Foro Italico *for any of the many sporting events that are hosted there (soccer, tennis, swimming, etc.), be sure to check out* Stadio dei Marmi *(Stadium of Marbles), so named because it is ringed with 60 four-meter-tall statues of impressively muscular athletes. It's a fun place to go for a run!*

www.eurspa.it

www.luneurpark.it

www.museocivilta.beniculturali.it

www.museociviltaromana.it

Verano Cemetery

Ancient Romans buried their dead outside the city walls to conserve limited space and mitigate the spread of diseases. As a result, many roads leading from Rome are lined for miles by mausoleums, catacombs, and the more modest graves of peasants and enslaved people. In the Middle Ages, the city's burial rules were relaxed, as illustrated by the tombs of the wealthy and powerful inside Rome's churches. By the early 19th century, however, burial was again restricted to outside the walls, and *Cimitero del Verano* was designated as an official city cemetery.

Consecrated in 1835, Verano was the primary cemetery for Rome for 150 years. Located adjacent to the San Lorenzo neighborhood, the cemetery contains over five million interments packed into 83 hectares of land accessed by gridded streets and walkways. It has special sections for clergy, children, WWI casualties, and a memorial to the Jews deported from Rome to Germany during WWII. The cemetery is mostly full, currently

accepting only those with reservations or whose life "brought honor" to the city of Rome.

Why go? The "Communal Monumental Cemetery of Campo Verano" lives up to its official name as soon as you pass through the front gate. Ornate memorial sculptures and family mausoleums line the streets and walkways closest to the entrance. Indeed, the city celebrates the rich heritage of the art in the cemetery by promoting it as an open-air museum. Farther back are row after row of multi-storied communal mausoleums, many fronted with the photographs of the people interred. There are so many hidden stories of lives lived. It is a very humbling experience.

 Where? The Verano Cemetery is just over 3 kilometers east of *Piazza Venezia*. The closest subway stop is Policlinico on the B Line, but it is still about a kilometer away. The 3 and 19 trams stop right in front of the cemetery.

 Cost and time? Everyone is allowed into the cemetery for FREE. The place is huge and it's relatively easy to get turned around. It's possible to spend several hours walking around because the different sections of the cemetery have very different characters.

 Kids? Not really. The subject matter is a little dark for most kids.

 Guide? As you would imagine, there are many well-known people buried in Verano. The cemetery has online brochures for self-guided tours to the graves of the famous based on themes including Italian cinema, patriots of the Italian Republic, and important women. Check online before you go or look for the QR codes on the posters at the cemetery entrance.

 When? Verano is open every day of the week, and they're serious about allowing entrance only until an hour before closing time, which is 6 pm in the winter and 7 pm in the summer.

FUN FACTS

✳ Portions of Verano were damaged by the Allied bombing of the San Lorenzo neighborhood during WWII.

✳ The Verano Cemetery is only the second-largest cemetery in Rome. The Flaminio-Prima Porta Cemetery, which is north of the city, covers roughly 130 hectares.

~~~~~~

Enrichment: The Basilica of San Lorenzo Outside the Walls, which is adjacent to Verano Cemetery, is one of the seven churches that pilgrims visit during the Easter Holy Week and Jubilee Years. The church namesake, Saint Lawrence, was martyred in the 3rd century AD when he angered the Roman tax collector by pointing to the poor people he aided through charity as the true untaxable treasure. He was then literally grilled over an open fire, apparently proclaiming "I'm done on this side, turn me over!" He later became the patron saint of cooks and comedians.

www.cimitericapitolini.it/english-version/list-of-cemeteries/79-the-verano -monumental-cemetery.html

ADVENTURE #XLV

Soratte Bunker in Sant'Oreste

Benito Mussolini wanted a place to feel safe in case something really bad happened, so in 1937 he had a tunnel built into the side of *Monte Soratte* that had room enough for his entire government. At the time it was the biggest bunker in the world at about 4 kilometers long. He never got the chance to use it, however, but when the Germans came to occupy Italy in 1943 under Field Marshal Kesselring, it became the German headquarters in central Italy after their previous HQ in Frascati was bombed. Indeed, the

Soratte Bunker withstood an allied bombing on May 12, 1944. Following WWII, the bunker was all but abandoned until it was secretly retrofitted in 1967 in response to the nuclear stresses of the Cold War. Today, the facility is owned by the Municipality of Sant'Oreste, which opens the bunker to the public through a local cultural association.

Why go? There is so much important 20th century history tied to this one big hole in the ground: Mussolini as a fascist leader, German occupation of Italy in WWII, and surviving the threat of a nuclear holocaust. There are not many places that combine insight into those events with a unique spelunking experience. And it's literally very cool in there!

 Where? The Soratte Bunker is 38 kilometers north of central Rome. It will take about an hour and 15 minutes to drive there. It's a 500-meter walk from the parking lot to the bunker. A train goes to Sant'Oreste from Rome-Flaminio roughly ten times a day, but the bunker on the hill is still a short bus or taxi ride from the train station in the valley.

Cost and time? Entry into the bunker is through a reserved guided tour. The cost is €10/adult. The tours occur on one weekend per month and take approximately two hours.

Kids? Kids under six years old are FREE, but there is no accommodation made for children on the tour. Teens and tweens will likely find the bunker pretty awesome.

Guide? All of the tour guides at the bunker are energetic volunteers with a passion for their local history. They will attempt to make an accommodation for English speakers.

When? Really, the best time to go to the bunker is anytime that you can get a tour reservation, but it's a particularly welcome escape from hot summer days. On the days that its open, there are usually two tours per day (10:30 and 15:30).

FUN FACTS

* Bring something warm to wear because the temperature drops inside the bunker, even in the middle of August. You should also bring a flashlight.
* The retrofit of the bunker for nuclear war also made it resistant to earthquakes.
* There is a rumor that some of the 72 tons of gold that Kesselring looted from the Bank of Italy is still lost somewhere in the bunker.

Enrichment: *The anniversary of the bombing of the bunker is commemorated on the weekend closest to May 12th, including historic reenactments with period uniforms, vehicles, and food. There are many other sites in this book related to Mussolini, including* Villa Torlonia, Villa Ada, *and EUR.*

☰ www.bunkersoratte.it

Anzio Beachhead Museum

More than 75 years later, the coastal town of Anzio is still mostly known as the site of an extremely costly WWII battle. Trying to drive the German army into retreat, Allied forces landed on the beaches of Anzio on January 22, 1944. After being bogged down for five devastating months, the Allies finally broke through and made their way to Rome, only 50 kilometers away. The Anzio Beachhead Museum (*Museo dello Sbarco*) commemorates the siege with historic items and first-hand stories of the time. It was inaugurated on the 50th anniversary of the Allied landing in 1994 and is housed in the 17th-century *Villa Adele*.

Why go? The museum is small but packed full of artifacts and memorabilia from one of the biggest turning points in the Allied war against the Germans in Italy. There are photos and maps and examples of uniforms

and weapons. But perhaps the most moving exhibits in the museum are the personal testimonials of the soldiers' experience living through impossibly harrowing times. Nearby to the museum are four military cemeteries worth visiting: two with primarily servicemen from Commonwealth countries (the Beach Head War Cemetery and the Anzio War Cemetery with 2,316 and 1,056 graves, respectively), one for American soldiers (Sicily-Rome American Cemetery and Memorial with 7,860 graves), and one for Germans killed at many places in southern Italy (*Cimitero Militare Tedesco* in Pomezia, with 27,443 graves).

 Where? Anzio is 51 kilometers south of central Rome on the Mediterranean coast. It will take a little over an hour to drive there. There is also a train that runs from Rome-Termini to Anzio about 15 times per day and takes about the same amount of time. It's walking distance from the Anzio station to the museum. The American cemetery is also walking distance from the next train station at Nettuno.

 Cost and time? Admission to the museum and cemeteries is FREE. The time needed at the museum and cemeteries will depend on your engagement with the topic.

 Kids? The theme of this adventure is quite somber but very important for remembering our relatively recent traumatic history.

 Guide? Not necessarily.

 When? The museum is open on Tuesdays, Thursdays, and Fridays, and with reservations on Saturdays and Sundays. Check on the website to make sure it's open when you want to go.

* Following the Allied invasion of Sicily in early July of 1943, Mussolini's fascist regime soon fell and he was arrested by his own king. The Germans immediately moved troops into northern Italy, while the succeeding Italian government surrendered to the Allies. When the Germans continued to move south on the Italian peninsula, with the Allies moving north, it set the stage for the battle of Anzio.

* The battle of Anzio has been the subject of many film documentaries, and a dramatic movie starring Robert Mitchum (*Anzio*, 1968).

* The father of Roger Waters, the bass player for Pink Floyd, died in the battle at Anzio and was an inspiration for the band's album *The Wall* (1979), which was subsequently made into a movie (1982).

Enrichment: *Emperor Nero, the 5th Roman emperor, was born in Anzio in 37 AD. Ruins of his villa above the beach at Anzio can be visited, as well as an archeological museum that is also located in* Villa Adele.

≡ www.sbarcodianzio.it

ADVENTURE #XLVII

The Great Mosque of Rome

Rome is home to one of the biggest Islamic mosques in Europe. The Great Mosque of Rome (*Grande Moschea di Roma*) can accommodate over 12,000 worshipers, with a main hall alone large enough for 2,500 people. The building, which combines both traditional and modern sensibilities, was designed by Sami Mousawi and Paolo Portoghesi and completed in 1995. It draws an international community of Muslims for the Friday Islamic holy day.

goodfreephotos.com

Why go? After seeing so many Catholic churches throughout Rome, it is refreshing to see a diversity of worshiping traditions and religious architecture. The outside of the mosque is quite grand with a single minaret and courtyards opening out into the surrounding trees. Inside, the support columns harken to a grove of palm trees, and there is extensive mosaic tiling on the walls and soft Persian carpets on the floor. How the sunlight penetrates into the building plays an important role in its ambience. The Muslim community welcomes visitors of all faiths to share the beauty of the space.

 Where? The mosque is 4.5 kilometers north-northeast of *Piazza Venezia*, and just west of *Villa Ada*. On Fridays there is a special bus route (230) to bring worshipers to the mosque from the nearby train station (*Campi Sportivi*).

 Cost and time? Prearranged tours are FREE and take about an hour. Everyone who visits the mosque is expected to wear appropriately modest attire, including headscarves for women.

Kids? Of course. Much of the outreach conducted by the mosque community is to raise awareness of Islam across the wider Roman world, including school groups. Your kids' interest in religious diversity may grow with exposure.

 Guide? Public entrance to the mosque is only through their in-house guided tours.

 When? The mosque is only open to the non-Muslim public on Wednesday and Saturday mornings.

FUN FACTS

* There are roughly 1.9 million Muslims in Italy, compared to about 41 million Catholics.
* Though many of the Muslims in Italy are recent immigrants, there has been a Muslim presence in Italy since the 9th century AD.

Enrichment: *Outside the mosque on Friday mornings, in conjunction with the Islamic holy day, there is a vibrant Arabic food market.* Mercato Esquilino *is a large indoor market near* Piazza Vittorio *that has stalls selling food and clothes from all over the world. The* Museo delle Civiltà *(Museum of Civilizations) in EUR explores the anthropology, archaeology, and history of non-European people and cultures.*

www.facebook.com/centroislamicoculturale
www.mercatidautore.com/en/mercati/esquilino/
www.museocivilta.beniculturali.it

PART TWO

Artful Adventures

Classics

Doria Pamphilj Gallery

The *Galleria Doria Pamphilj* (not a typo) contains the private art collection of the Doria Pamphilj family. Much of the historic wealth of the family stems from Pope Innocent X (né Pamphilj), who was head of the church from 1644 to 1655. He and his sister-in-law, Olimpia Maidalchini, were able to grow a fortune that was used to develop this collection. Much of the art is from the 16th and 17th centuries and includes works by Velazquez, Caravaggio, Bernini, the Bruegels, and Raphael.

Why go? There are really two stars here, the art in the gallery and the palace where the gallery is located. The gallery begins on the second floor of the palazzo by entering through a grand entrance hall—two stories of large windows and even larger paintings. Then there are royal apartments, furniture, a stunning ballroom, and a chapel before the focus shifts back to paintings and sculpture. The rooms where the entire wall space is given over to paintings of various shapes and sizes are amazing.

 Where? The entrance to the gallery is 150 meters up *Via del Corso* from *Piazza Venezia*, in the center of everything.

 Cost and time? Tickets to the gallery cost €15/person and should be reserved ahead of time (see their website). People are let into the gallery in discrete groups at two-hour intervals. Each group must leave before the next group is allowed to enter.

 Kids? Though some kids will love to see the inside of the palazzo, most little kids will need a task stay engaged—perhaps counting all the dogs in the paintings? Teenagers may be intrigued by the golden age of papal wealth and might find the first-person audio guide of the apartment interesting.

 Guide? Admission includes an audio guide narrated by current members of the Doria Pamphilj family, which provides a fascinating window into their world, both past and present.

 When? The museum is open everyday from 10 am to 8 pm with a reservation. Check the website for updated information. This museum is often one of the few open on Mondays.

FUN FACTS

* Listen on the audio guide for when the present-day Doria Pamphiljs speak about Olimpia Maidalchini and how they are still benefiting from her shrewd business deals.

* Other properties once owned and named after the Doria Pamphilj family include *Villa Doria Pamphilj*, a major city park on the west side of Rome, and *Palazzo Pamphilj*, a palace on *Piazza Navona* that is now home to the Brazilian Embassy (tours by reservation through their website).

Enrichment: *The Café Doria (at* Via della Gatta 1*) on the backside of the palace has some excellent post-museum desserts. Other palaces and villas in Rome that are art galleries open to the public include* Galleria Borghese, Galleria Colonna, Palazzo Barberini, *and* Palazzo Corsini.

www.doriapamphilj.it/roma/
www.ambasciatadelbrasile.it/palacio/visita_guidata.asp

ADVENTURE #XLIX

Palazzo Barberini

The *Palazzo Barberini* is a palace built in the early 17th century by Maffeo Barberini, who would later become Pope Urban VIII. The villa is known for its architecture and amazing frescoes, particularly the staircases and painting on the ceiling of the central salon. Today, it is home to half of the National Gallery of Ancient Art (*Galleria Nazionale d'Arte Antica*), and houses paintings by Raphael, Caravaggio, and El Greco, among many others.

Why go? Like all the beautiful noble residences turned into public art galleries, there are two things to see here: the art and the palace itself. Put them together and it is truly stunning, with amazing paintings highlighted in gorgeous rooms. There is a separate guided tour of the apartments on the top floor, two unforgettable stairways, and a pleasant garden in the back of the palace.

 Where? *Palazzo Barberini* is only a kilometer northeast of *Piazza Venezia*. The palace is on a block bookended by *Piazza Barberini* on one side and the Four Fountains (*Quattro Fontane*) intersection on the other. There is a self-named subway stop in the piazza, which is on the A Line. But if you walked here from *Piazza Venezia* you would pretty much have to pass by the Trevi Fountain.

 Cost and time? Seeing the palace and the museum will take at least a couple of hours. The entrance fee for the museum is €10/person. The ticket is also good for the second half of the museum, which is housed in *Palazzo Corsini* (see Adventure #L), but is valid for only 20 days.

 Kids? Teenagers, and maybe tweens, might appreciate the history and beauty of the place, but the younger kids will have more fun spotting the cats in the garden.

 Guide? Yes, the stories of both the art and the palace would be more fascinating if told by an expert.

 When? *Palazzo Barberini* is open Tuesdays to Sundays. Go on a rainy day or a hot summer afternoon.

FUN FACTS

＊ Don't miss Corradini's statue of the "Veiled Woman," which captures her facial features underneath the veil — it's astounding!

✳ Caravaggio is a master of chiaroscuro, or creating contrasts of light and shadow in his paintings.

✳ A second century AD Mithraeum, or temple dedicated to Mithra, was rediscovered behind Palazzo Barberini in 1936.

~~~~~~~~~~~~~~~~~~~~~~~~~~

Enrichment: After the palace, go see the nearby fountains: *Quattro Fontane* at the intersection of *Via delle Quattro Fontane* and *Via del Quirinale*, and the Bernini fountains, *Fontana del Tritone* and *Fontana delle Api*, in *Piazza Barberini*. Other palaces and villas to visit for their art include *Villa Farnesina*, *Palazzo Braschi*, and *Palazzo Altemps*.

≡ www.barberinicorsini.org/en/

ADVENTURE #L

Palazzo Corsini

Palazzo Corsini is a baroque palace on the Trastevere side of the river. The original structure was built by Cardinal Raffaele Riario in 1511, and significantly updated in the mid-1600s by Queen Christina of Sweden, who had abdicated her throne to become Catholic and move to Rome. Cardinal Lorenzo Corsini, from Florence, became Pope Clement XII in 1730, and his family bought the villa in 1736. The Pope's nephew, Cardinal Neri Maria Corsini, soon expanded the palace to what it is today. The family sold *Palazzo Corsini* to the Italian government in 1883 and donated their accumulated art collection, creating Italy's first national art gallery. Today it houses half of the National Gallery of Ancient Art (*Galleria Nazionale d'Arte Antica*), along with *Palazzo Barberini*.

The gardens behind *Palazzo Corsini* were combined with the Papal Herbal Garden in 1883 to become the Botanical Garden of Rome (*Orto Botanico di Roma*), currently administered by La Sapienza University. The gardens extend up Janiculum Hill and have over 3,000 plant species and historic greenhouses.

Why go? Similar to *Palazzo Barberini*, *Palazzo Corsini* offers the awesome juxtaposition of a beautiful palace with classic 16th and 17th century art. It has works by Caravaggio, Reni, van Dyck, and Rubens, among many others. The gardens are also worth a visit, as a quiet oasis from city life.

Where? The palace is less than 1,500 meters west of *Piazza Venezia*, but on the other side of the Tiber River. It's about a 20-minute walk, about the same amount of time it would take you to find and ride a bus. There is no nearby subway station.

Cost and time? Getting into the museum will cost €10/person, and the ticket is also good for the *Palazzo Barberini* if used within 20 days. The botanical garden costs €4/person. The museum and garden will probably take at least half a day to visit.

Gallerie Nazionali di Arte Antica, Roma (MiC) Bibliotheca Hertziana Istituto Max Planck per la storia dell'arte/Enrico Fontolan

Kids? The entrance fee for the museum is FREE for anyone under 18, but younger kids will probably enjoy running around the garden more. The botanical garden is also FREE for anyone under 6 years old.

Guide? Helpful, but not necessary.

When? In the spring and summer, when the garden is at its best. Visit the gardens in the morning and the museum during the heat of the day.

FUN FACTS

* *Palazzo Corsini* is also home to the *Accademia Nazionale dei Lincei* (literally the "National Academy of the Lynx-eyed"), which was founded in 1603 as a scientific academy and currently still promotes and funds various scientific research. Galileo Galilei, the father of modern physics and the scientific method, was a member of the academy.
* Every day at the top of Janiculum Hill, immediately above the botanical garden behind *Palazzo Corsini*, soldiers fire a cannon to mark the noon hour. Started by Pope Pius IX in 1847 to standardize the ringing of church bells, it's been happening at this location since 1904, except during WWII and its aftermath.

Enrichment: *Just across the street from* Palazzo Corsini *is the* Villa Farnesina, *which became the prototype for the new Renaissance villa and has impressive frescoes.*

www.barberinicorsini.org/en/
www.ortobotanicoitalia.it/lazio/romalasapienza/
web.uniroma1.it/ortobotanico/en

Roman Churches

There are rumored to be over 900 churches in the city of Rome, of which 66 are Catholic basilicas granted special status by the Pope. After Constantine the Great ceased the persecution of Christians in Rome in 313 AD, churches sprang up in all quarters, often in commemoration of a saint or a martyr. Of course, there are the big four basilicas that most people come to Rome to see (St. Peter's, St. John in Lateran, St. Mary Major, and St. Paul Outside the Walls), but there are so many others that are almost equally as grand, with amazing frescoes, paintings, mosaics, statues, and colorful marble from all over the world.

Why go? Though some of the churches in Rome are austere, most are quite opulent. The oldest ones are roughly 1,700 years old, but they've probably been refurbished once or twice over the centuries. Many of the paintings and sculptures inside are by famous artists or their disciples. Works by Caravaggio, Bernini, Raphael, and Michelangelo can all be found in the churches of Rome, even in small out-of-the-way places. There are also tons of great art inside the churches by artists you've probably never heard of. Even if you are not Catholic, or religious at all, churches are still excellent places to duck into for a little calm, quiet, and contemplation — or simply a cool oasis on a warm day.

 Where? Wherever you are in Rome, you aren't that far from an amazing church. When you're on your way somewhere else, if you have the time, just pop in that open door and see what's inside. It may take only a couple of minutes, and it's a good bet you will experience something historic and beautiful.

 Cost and time? Entering most Catholic churches in Rome is FREE. Typically only museums or special exhibits associated with

churches charge entrance fees. Bring some coins because many churches will temporarily brighten their most prized paintings with light vending machines.

Kids? Probably not. Catholic imagery can be pretty brutal, but this might be a plus for the teens. If that's the case, check out *Santo Stefano Rotondo*, which has many frescoes portraying various scenes of martyrdom, *Chiesa dell'Orazione e Morte*, which has a chamber decorated with human bones, or go straight to *Santa Maria della Concezione dei Cappuccini*, the church above the Capuchin Crypt.

Guide? Old churches are more interesting the more you know about them, so a guide would bring them to life. But that shouldn't stop you from going in to explore for yourself.

 When? Anytime you are passing by a church that you haven't been in yet.

FUN FACTS

* Religious relics, mainly in the form of the human bones of saints, have been big business for centuries. Many churches have altars constructed around relics of a patron saint that often have colorful stories about how they came to be where they are. Relics seem to add legitimacy to churches and attract pilgrims, who bring their tourist spending money.

* A pilgrimage to seven churches, including the four major basilicas, still takes place. It was traditionally conducted on Ash Wednesday but is now held on a day in May and a day in September (see the website for the Santa Maria in Vallicella Church for their calendar of events). It takes a full day to walk to all of them, but the time can be shortened significantly with a bicycle.

Enrichment: *The Caravaggio tour of his paintings in churches in central Rome (ask your guide) includes* Santa Maria del Popolo, San Luigi dei Francesi, *and the Basilica of Sant'Agostino. The Bernini sculpture tour of churches includes* San Francesco a Ripa, Basilica di San Sebastiano, *and* Santa Maria della Vittoria. *Making lists like this is really endless.*

www.afriendinrome.it/?p=3293

www.wantedinrome.com/news/where-to-see-caravaggio-paintings-in-rome
.html

www.vallicella.org

Villa Farnesina

Built in the early 16th century by Agostino Chigi, a successful business-man and the treasurer to Pope Julius II, *Villa Farnesina* was originally envisioned as a kind of suburban summer house on the Tiber River. Chigi commissioned frescoes by a host of well-known artists, including Raphael and Peruzzi. The villa came under the ownership of the Farnese family in 1577 and was so named to distinguish it from other Farnese properties. Michelangelo suggested building a bridge across the Tiber to link the villa to *Palazzo Farnese* directly on the other side, but that never happened. After a century-long stint belonging to a Spanish Ambassador to Naples, the villa has been owned by the Italian Government since 1927.

Why go? At the time, *Villa Farnesina* became the prototype for a new Renaissance villa: not too large, a beautiful interior with fantastic fres-coes, and overlooking a garden that went down to the river. Today, a few rooms are typically open to visitors, but they contain the true stars of the villa, which are the recently restored frescoes. Some utilize trompe l'oeil to deceive the viewer into thinking the paintings are three dimensional, including a ceiling that looks like a hanging tapestry. There are also the astrological ceiling, period landscapes, and images that harken to a history of love between nobility and commoners.

 Where? *Villa Farnesina* is less than 1.5 kilometers west of *Piazza Venezia*, but on the other side of the Tiber River in the Trastevere neighborhood. There is no nearby subway station, though there is a bus stop right outside along *Lungotevere della Farnesina*.

 Cost and time? An "ordinary" ticket to *Villa Farnesina* costs €10/adult. There is also a €12 ticket that includes a guided tour of the garden, and an €18 ticket that includes a concert of

Renaissance music (but only on the 2nd Sunday of the month).
Seeing both the villa and its garden will take a couple of hours.
A ticket to the Vatican Museums gets the bearer a discount on their
ticket to *Villa Farnesina* if used within seven days.

Kids? If your kids are into classic wall and ceiling paintings, then they will love this place.

 Guide? An audio guide to *Villa Farnesina* is available for €3, and tours of the garden are conducted by an internal villa guide.

 When? Since visiting Villa Farnesina has both indoor and outdoor components, go on a day when the weather is good.

FUN FACTS

* Chigi may have been the richest man in the world in his day. Legend has it that when hosting elaborate dinner parties at the villa he threw the dirty silver plates and cutlery into the Tiber River, in a display of ostentatious wealth. He wasn't stupid, however, and had nets positioned downstream to catch his own booty.

* Painting on recently laid plaster allows a fresco to merge with the plaster as it sets, becoming an integral part of the wall.

* *Villa Farnesina*, along with *Palazzo Corsini*, holds official functions for the *Accademia Nazionale dei Lincei*, a "keen-eyed" scientific academy that promotes and funds research on everything from geology to political science.

Enrichment: Palazzo Corsini *is across the street from* Villa Farnesina *and* Palazzo Farnese *is directly across the river. Both palaces are also fantastic examples of Renaissance architecture and art and definitely worth a visit. Also in the immediate neighborhood is the Botanical Garden of Rome and Janiculum Hill. Another beautiful art and architecture project funded by the Chigi family is their namesake chapel in the Basilica of Santa Maria del Popolo, which was designed by Raphael and decorated by Bernini.*

≡ www.villafarnesina.it/?lang=en

Palazzo Colonna

Undoubtedly built on ruins from ancient Rome, the *Palazzo Colonna* dates back to the 12th century AD and is one of the oldest and largest palaces still in private ownership in Rome. Constantly morphing and changing through the centuries, the palazzo has been home to the Colonna family for over 800 years. The family included Pope Martin V, whose election in 1417 effectively ended the Avignon Schism and reestablished the Papacy back in Rome. In 1527, the palace avoided being sacked by troops loyal to the Holy Roman Empire largely because of the family's alliance with the Hapsburgs. Today, an amazingly beautiful gallery at the palace displays the extensive art collected by the family over the years. The public can also visit a royal apartment, which includes frescoes and period furniture, and the gardens, which are accessible from the palace via four small bridges over *Via della Pilotta*.

Why go? The *Galleria Colonna* displays over 250 priceless paintings by dozens of master artists in a stunning palatial setting. The Great Hall has been compared in beauty to the galleries of Versailles. It is amazing! The apartment is named after Princess Isabelle, a beloved family matriarch who died in 1984. She was the last of a very long line of the Colonna family to live in the regal rooms. The garden has pretty waterfalls, relics from ancient Rome, and stunning views of the city.

 Where? The *Palazzo Colonna* is only 100 meters east of *Piazza Venezia* along *Via Cesare Battisti*. The entrance is in *Via della Pilotta*.

 Cost and time? Entrance to the three palace attractions — the *galleria*, apartments, and garden — requires separate tickets. An adult ticket to each of the three sites individually is €12/15/10,

respectively, or can be purchased together for €30. Just the galleria and apartment is €25, and the galleria and garden is €20. It will take several hours, if not the whole morning, to see everything.

Kids? The beauty is stunning and can be appreciated by all ages. Kids will especially get a kick out of imagining what it might be like to live in that apartment.

 Guide? Yes. With so much family history tied to this place, it would be most interesting to hear it from a guide. Entrance to the garden is only allowed with an in-house guided tour.

 When? The opening times of the palace are complicated. Though the palace is officially open to the public only on Saturday mornings, arranging access with your own tour guide is possible, for an extra cost, on any day of the week. The gardens are only open on Saturday mornings.

FUN FACTS

* During the short life of the Roman Republic in 1849, a cannonball was fired from Janiculum Hill by the French Army that landed on the stairs leading to the Great Hall in the *Galleria Colonna*. It is still there.
* Perhaps the most famous painting in the gallery is *The Bean-Eater* by Annibale Carracci, because few Italian painters of the time illustrated the common man doing mundane things.
* *Palazzo Colonna* appears in the final press conference scene of *Roman Holiday* (1953), starring Audrey Hepburn and Gregory Peck.

Enrichment: The palace is in the center of the city and walking distance to the Victor Emmanuel II Monument, Trevi Fountain, and the Colosseum.

☰ www.galleriacolonna.it/en/

Santo Stefano Rotondo

The first thing that you need to know about *Santo Stefano Rotondo*, also known as the *Basilica di Santo Stefano al Monte Celio*, is that it was one of the first churches in Rome, having been built in the mid-5th century AD, to have a circular floor plan. The second thing to know about the church is that its circular interior walls are lined with three-dozen frescoes depicting some very gruesome methods of becoming a martyr. The paintings are from the 16th century, and show early Christians being grilled, torn apart by horses, and eaten by wild animals, among many other tortures.

Why go? Yes, the church is structurally special. But if you thought that seeing Jesus crucified on a cross every time you walked into a Catholic church isn't startling enough, then this is definitely the place for you.

 Where? *Santo Stefano Rotondo* is less than 2 kilometers southeast of *Piazza Venezia*. A couple of bus routes (81 and 673) stop out front.

 Cost and time? The church is FREE and it won't take more than an hour to get totally spooked!

 Kids? Certainly the teens and tweens will be fascinated and grossed out by the frescoes. It is probably too explicit for the younger kids.

 Guide? Yes, finding out why the church wants to depict acts of martyrdom so graphically needs an explaination. Were the victims all sainted for becoming martyrs?

 When? Like other spooky adventures in this book (e.g., the Capuchin Crypt, the catacombs), going to this church might be at its most impressive around Halloween.

FUN FACTS

* Theoretically, the frescoes were commissioned in the time of the Reformation (i.e., protestant challenges to papal authority) to prepare German seminary students from the neighboring college for what to expect when they returned home: a literal suicide mission!
* Each painting has an inscription identifying the emperor responsible for the depicted torture.
* Charles Dickens was impressed enough by the paintings to write about *Santo Stefano Rotondo* on his visit to Rome in 1846.

Enrichment: *To enhance the possibility of nightmares, you can explore the brotherhood of the* Sacconi Rossi, *who collected human bones in a crypt on Tiberina Island in the 18th and 19th centuries, similar to the Capuchin Crypt. They still do a night procession in their red robes on All Souls Day (November 2nd). Or to avoid the nightmares, change the subject with a visit to the public garden at* Villa Celimontana, *just across the street.*

☰ www.cgu.it/it/santo-stefano-rotondo/

Tempietto del Bramante

The story goes that Saint Peter was crucified upside down on the southern end of Janiculum Hill in 64 AD, during the reign of Emperor Nero. To commemorate the suspected site of the crucifixion, the Church of San Pietro in Montorio was built on the site in the late 15th century, replacing an earlier church structure that dated back to the 9th century. Inside a small courtyard of the church, Donato Bramante built a small circular temple over the purported actual spot of Saint Peter's martyrdom. It was completed in the early 1500s and became known as *Tempietto del Bramante* (Little Temple by Bramante).

Why go? The Little Temple is considered an early prototype for Saint Peter's Basilica, which Bramante also designed, and one of the most beautiful, significant examples of Renaissance architecture. It has perfect cylindrical proportions with columns, niches, and a dome. There is a hole in the crypt of the temple signifying where the crucifix was planted. There is also an accompanying small museum.

 Where? The temple is less than 2 kilometers southwest of *Piazza Venezia*, perched partway up Janiculum Hill from Trastevere. There is a bus stop (Garibaldi/Iacobucci) on route 115 just out in front.

 Cost and time? To get in to see the *Tempietto* is FREE. It is, by name, quite small so it won't take more than an hour to visit.

 Kids? Though the architecture is very attractive, images of crucifixion are not terribly kid-friendly, especially when the victim is hanging by his feet.

 Guide? Yes, but because of the small size of the temple, any tour should also include nearby sights as well.

When? The temple is closed on Mondays, but the view through the closed gates is still spectacular.

FUN FACTS

✳ Bramante got his start in Urbino and Milan before moving to Rome. He was also a painter and a poet.

✳ The construction of the Church of San Pietro in Montorio and the *Tempietto* were commissioned by the King and Queen of Spain.

✳ The Academy of Spain (*Accademia di Spagna*) found a permanent home in the convent adjoining the church in 1876, where it is still located today. There is often an art exhibition by an academy fellow included with the entrance to the *Tempietto*.

Enrichment: A scene from the 2013 movie La Grande Bellezza *(*The Great Beauty*), which won an Academy Award for the Best Foreign Language Film, was filmed inside the* Tempietto. *There are many sights along Janiculum Hill including* Fontana dell'Acqua Paola, *monuments to Garibaldi and his wife Anita, 84 statues of prominent Italians, and an overlook of the city. Every day at noon, a cannon is fired from just below the overlook terrace to mark the time. Downhill from the* Tempietto, *it is a short distance to* Palazzo Corsini, *the Botanical Garden, and* Villa Farnesina. *Bramante's first architectural work in Rome is the cloister in the Church of Santa Maria della Pace near* Piazza Navona.

☰ www.accademiaspagna.org

Modern

The National Gallery of Modern and Contemporary Art

The *Galleria Nazionale d'Arte Moderna e Contemporanea* (GNAM) displays paintings and sculpture from the 19th to 21st centuries, from both their extensive regular collection and dynamic special exhibits. There are works here by well-known Italians like de Chirico, Corcos, and Boccioni, as well as many international stars. The Palace of Fine Art, which houses the museum, has beautiful large galleries and was completed in 1915.

Why go? The National Gallery of Modern and Contemporary Art fills the sweet spot between classical Renaissance art found in *Galleria Borghese* and elsewhere, and the edgier modern art found at the MAXXI.

 Where? The museum is 2.5 kilometers north of *Piazza Venezia*. Flaminio is the closest subway stop to the museum on the A Line. From there it's a 600-meter walk through *Villa Borghese*, or transfer to the 2 tram and then the 19 tram. The 3 tram also stops right in front of the museum.

 Cost and time? Admission into the museum is €10/person, though there is a discount if you have a recent ticket to the MAXXI. The museum is quite large and will generally take a couple of hours to see.

 Kids? Tweens and teens will have lots to keep them interested in this museum, but littler kids might need a sketch pad and colored pencils to stay engaged.

 Guide? Not necessary, although there's usually way more to the story of a painting than meets the eye, which a guide could explain.

 When? The best time to visit any indoor museum is on a rainy day, or in the afternoon of a summer day to escape from the heat.

FUN FACTS

* In many of the galleries there is an interesting juxtaposition of modern paintings with more classical-style sculptures.
* A painting by Gustav Klimt, *The Three Ages of Woman*, hangs in GNAM. The Italian Government acquired it in 1910, when Klimt was still alive.
* There is a seasonal outdoor bar at the top of the steps across the street. The café in the museum, which was one of the nicest museum cafés in the city, is temporarily closed.
* The lion sculptures on the steps to the entrance of the museum are awesome!

Enrichment: Villa Giulia, *a Renaissance villa home to the National Etruscan Museum, is just up the street from the art gallery.* Villa Borghese, *the best park in Rome with multiple attractions, is right across the street. If you are interested in the science of animals, the Museum of Zoology is also within walking distance.*

☰ www.lagallerianazionale.com/en

The MAXXI

MAXXI is the National Museum of 21st Century Art (a.k.a. The National Center for Contemporary Art and Architecture). Located in the Flaminio neighborhood in northern Rome, it displays their regular collection of modern art, hosts discussions of architecture, and includes an ever-changing array of special exhibits. The building itself, designed by Zaha Hadid, is one of the stars. There is also a gift shop and a café.

Why go? After being inundated with the classic sculptures of ancient Rome and paintings of the Renaissance, there is likely room in your artistic appetite for more current creative energy.

 Where? MAXXI is 4 kilometers north-northwest of *Piazza Venezia*. Take Line A to the Flaminio stop and then get on the 2 tram to the Apollodoro stop. The museum is then a block and a half west.

 Cost and time? The entrance fee for the museum €12/adult. There is also an annual pass for €50. The time it takes to tour the MAXXI will depend on your engagement, but probably not more than a couple of hours. Finding all the galleries in the museum labyrinth can be a challenge, but the café is a great place to end.

 Kids? Certainly, older teenagers can be engaged by contemporary art, but littler kids might need some guidance and art supplies for creating their own inspired works.

 Guide? No need for a guide for this one, but like other museums, there is always more to discover with an insiders' contribution.

 When? Bad weather days are a perfect time to go to an indoor museum. Closed on Mondays.

FUN FACTS

＊ Recent special exhibits have included a room full of mattresses, even on the ceiling, inviting patrons to take off their shoes and take a break, and an outdoor house open to the elements including all the furniture and assorted bric-a-brac.

＊ The MAXXI was built on the site of a former military barracks, and was awarded the prestigious Stirling Prize for excellence in architecture in 2010, the year it opened.

Enrichment: *In addition to MAXXI, there is also MACRO, the Museum of Contemporary Art of Rome, on* Via Nizza *near* Villa Torlonia. *It houses temporary exhibits and artist projects, among other things, and is FREE. It also has an excellent bar on the roof!*

www.maxxi.art/en/
www.museomacro.it

Centrale Montemartini

What to do with a long-obsolete electric power generating plant in an old industrial part of the city? Turn it into an art museum, of course! The *Centrale Montemartini*, named after a city councilor who died suddenly during a city council meeting, was the first public power plant in Rome and operated from 1912 until 1963. It sat dormant for a couple of decades until the power company decided to restore it into an art and multimedia center rather than demolish it, while keeping the historic machinery in place. After a hugely successful temporary exhibition of ancient Roman sculptures in the space in 1997, the exhibits were upgraded to a permanent museum in 2001. The museum is now part of the extensive system of Civic Museums of Rome, which includes 44 museums and archeological sites.

Why go? The juxtaposition of the archaic industrial machinery and the ancient statues is both startling and visually pleasing. There are roughly 400 high-quality white statues from both the republican and imperial ages of Rome intermingled with hulking metal contraptions. Descriptions of the function of the boilers and engines are contrasted with the stories of ancient archeological discovery. The place is just cool, mixing the very old with the merely obsolete.

 Where? *Centrale Montemartini* is roughly 3 kilometers south of *Piazza Venezia*, in the Ostiense neighborhood. The museum is walking distance from the Garbatella subway station on the B Line.

 Cost and time? The entry fee for the museum is €10/adult. There is also combination ticket (€16) for both *Centrale Montemartini* and *Musei Capitolini*. Residents of Rome qualify for the MIC card, which allows access to the Civic Museums in Rome for a year for only €5. A visit to the museum should take a couple of hours.

 Kids? For little kids, there's not much that will engage them except maybe for the Pope's train cars (see Fun Facts) and perhaps some really fun photo opps. But teenagers can appreciate the melding of art and technology from two vastly different periods of Rome's history.

 Guide? There are good descriptions of the statues and installations in the museum, but a guide would help extract the truly amazing and unique aspects of the many pieces.

 When? Since the entire museum is indoors and protected from the environment, go on a bad weather day.

FUN FACTS

✳ Included in the sculptures of the museum is a sarcophagus from the 2nd century AD of a young woman named Crepereia Tryphaena. She was buried with a unique ivory doll that has realistic articulated limbs. The doll is also on display.

✳ Seemingly a little out of place and kind of at the back of the museum is an old boiler room that contains several glitzy train cars made for Pope Pius IX in 1858 to travel between cities in the Papal States. They were only used until 1870, however, when Italian unification rendered the Papal States obsolete. The train cars are some of the oldest in Italy.

Enrichment: *Apart from the Basilica of Saint Paul Outside the Walls,* which is just south of Centrale Montemartini, *the* Via Ostiense/*Gasometer* side of the Ostiense neighborhood is currently undergoing an energetic renewal. Roma Tre University, rapidly growing on the other side of Via Ostiense *from the museum, now has more than 35,000 students. Part of its growth will eventually include the renovation of the large* Mercati Generali, *which has sat dormant for a couple of decades. There is also an active street mural initiative in this and other Roman neighborhoods.*

www.centralemontemartini.org

www.museiincomuneroma.it

Urban Murals

The urban mural or street art scene in Rome has evolved well past the ubiquitous and annoying "I-was-here" tagging and grade-schoolish graffiti. It has become a true art form and, for artists, a valid alternative to indoor gallery exhibition. Street art is difficult to classify due to its diversity in spatial scale, quality, and meaning. It runs the gamut from attempting to beautify the roller shutters on the front of closed shops to spanning whole walls on the exterior of five-story apartment buildings. There are literally thousands of murals throughout Rome in almost every neighborhood. Community organizations, including the Mayor's office, have encouraged urban murals as a way of transforming neighborhoods, giving them a tangible identity, and attracting people who wouldn't otherwise go there.

The neighborhoods that have murals worth visiting include Ostiense, San Lorenzo, San Basilio, Pigneto/Torpignattara, Quadraro, and Trullo. The street art scene in Rome includes festivals that attract famous international artists to create murals in neighborhood clusters or on a theme. The "Big City Life" project, for instance, sponsored the creation of 22 murals on 11 condo buildings in Tor Marancia. The many featured Italian artists include Alicè Pasquini, Blu, Maupal, and Solo.

Why go? Not all the art in Rome revolves around classic sculpture and Renaissance painting. This is an active and dynamic contemporary art scene that expands the edges of art while still being accessible to everyone. There are even organized walking, bicycle, and Vespa tours to help experience the diversity of Rome's street art.

 Where? Admittedly, the most vibrant street art in Rome tends toward the grittier neighborhoods, where they enhance the character, draw attention, and build community pride. All of the neighborhoods are on public transport, and an Internet search can produce maps of appropriate walking tours — or search for a "mural" near wherever you happen to be.

 Cost and time? Walking around the neighborhoods of Rome is FREE. You can walk until your feet get sore.

 Kids? Absolutely!

 Guide? Yes. Sometimes, even with a map, the murals can be difficult to find. A guide can save you from walking around the block again and offer information about the artist's motivation in creating the mural.

 When? It's all outside by definition, so go when the weather is good. Go in the daytime because few, if any, of the murals are lit for the nighttime. Whichever neighborhood you go to, you will likely discover a new bakery or gelateria too!

FUN FACTS

* An obsolete psychiatric hospital in northwest Rome, *Santa Maria della Piet*à, was converted into a 28-hectare city park in 2000. It now hosts over 30 murals.

* Following the earthquake that struck central Italy in 2016, 100 tour guides funded the development of murals in several Roman neighborhoods and host annual mural events to raise money for affected communities.

* There are at least a couple of galleries in Rome that specialize in the art of the same artists that produce urban murals and street art: Galleria Varsi and Wunderkammern.

Enrichment: *Have you ever heard of an ecomuseum? Imagine a map developed by a grassroots organization to highlight the many cool cultural values of their neighborhood. They are using the map as a tool to raise awareness of the threat of unwanted development that could destroy the fabric of their community. This is an ecomuseum; using the existing features in the cultural and physical landscape to advocate for their preservation. Beginning in the early 1970s, the ecomuseum idea has spread to roughly 300 cities worldwide. This includes* Ecomuseo Casilino Ad Duas Lauros, *which began in 2012 to protect a Roman neighborhood from building speculation. You, too, can download their map and take a walk in their shoes.*

www.turismoroma.it/wp-content/uploads/2015/04/leaflet_streetart.pdf

www.bigcitylife.it

www.murilab.it

www.murisicuri.it

www.galleriavarsi.it

www.wunderkammern.net

www.ecomuseocasilino.it

Cinecittà Studios

Welcome to Italy's Hollywood! Cinecittà is Europe's largest film studio and home to Italy's active movie industry. Many famous directors have made movies here including Federico Fellini, Sergio Leone, Francis Ford Coppola, and Wes Anderson. Originally founded by Benito Mussolini in 1937 to develop video propaganda, the studio is now a collection of active sound stages and outdoor movie sets of historic proportions.

Why go? There are three reasons to go to Cinecittà:

1. To learn about the history of Italian cinema. The studio museum (MIAC) is a fascinating walk through some of Italy's most famous films.

2. To learn about the art of filmmaking. The tour of the sound stages is a window into constructing a fantasy world on screen.

3. To gaze at the outdoor movie sets constructed to mimic ancient times.

 Where? Cinecittà is at the edge of Rome, 9 kilometers southeast of *Centro Storico*. It has its own subway stop near the end of the A Line going toward Anagnina.

 Cost and time? It costs €15/adult for admission to the museum, which includes a guided tour of the sound stages and movie sets.

Andrea Martella

There is a sliding scale for kids and students, as well as a family ticket. The whole visit takes a couple of hours, and there is a café and gift shop on site.

 Kids? Tweens and teens will love to see the fake historic buildings in the outdoor movie sets. Teens will appreciate the museum, particularly if they have had previous exposure to Italian movies.

 Guide? The tour of the sound stages and outdoor movie sets are guided by studio staff. Tours in Italian are available four times a day, and English-language tours are everyday at 11:30 am. Advanced booking is obligatory (visit@cinecittaluce.it). You can tour the studio museum at your own pace.

 When? The studio is open every day except Tuesdays. Since much of the tour is outside, avoid particularly hot or rainy days.

FUN FACTS

* Following WWII, film production ceased temporarily at Cinecittà partly because it had been bombed, but also because it became the home of 3,000 war refugees.
* Forty-seven movies filmed at Cinecittà have won an Academy Award.
* The word "paparazzi" is based on a news photographer character named Paparazzo in Federico Felini's *La Dolce Vita* (1960), which was filmed at Cinecittà.
* The studio is not to be confused with Cinecittà World, an amusement park on the outskirts of Rome.

Enrichment: Fellini had a special relationship with Cinecittà because, unlike many neorealists, he wanted to control the setting of many of his films. Watching any of his films before you go is sure to enrich your experience. Indeed, a memorial was held for him in Studio 5 after he died. Classic films like Ben-Hur *(1959),* La Dolce Vita *(1960),* Cleopatra *(1963), and* Romeo and Juliet *(1968) were filmed here, as were* The English Patient *(1996) and* The Life Aquatic with Steve Zissou *(2004). Scenes from the HBO series* Rome *(2004) were also filmed here.*

www.cinecittastudios.it

www.cinecittasimostra.it/en/opening-hours-and-prices/

www.museomiac.it/en/

ADVENTURE #LXI

Outdoor Cinema

In the summertime in Rome, one of best parts of the day is when the sun is setting, making everything look yellow and orange. The intensity of the day's heat dissipates as the Romans emerge from the shade to enjoy the social fabric of the city. One of the popular summer evening activities is for people to join their friends at one of the many outdoor movie cinemas. The most well-known outdoor cinemas are in *Villa Borghese* (*Casa del Cinema*) and on Tiberina Island (*L'Isola del Cinema*), but there is also a seasonal theater in the Aqueduct Park (Cinecittà Film Festival) and sometimes a "Floating Theater" in *Parco Centrale del Lago* in EUR. Of course, most of the films are shown in Italian, but many foreign movies are presented in their native language accompanied by Italian subtitles.

Why go? The movies shown at most of the outdoor cinemas are curated to highlight a theme, a director, or an actor, effectively making them mini film festivals. Some have reserved seating and some require you to bring your own chair; some serve food and drinks; some also include musical entertainment. It's just a fantastic way to spend a summer evening under the stars.

 Where? Outdoor cinemas are all over the city. Apart from the ones already mentioned, they also include Cinema Tiziano (*Via*

Guido Reni 2), *Arena Garbatella* (*Piazza Benedetto Brin*), *Arena Adriano* Studios (*Via Tiburtina 521*), and *Arena Nuovo Sacher* (*Largo Ascianghi 1*). And don't forget *Il Cinema in Piazza*, which takes place in three different places: *Piazza San Cosimato*, *Monte Ciocci* in Valle Aurelia, and *Casale della Cervelletta* in Tor Sapienza. Obviously, check their websites for details before you set out, including the cinema locations that tend to change from year to year.

Being in the city means that the cinemas will generally be in close proximity to public transportation. Getting home after the movie may require a taxi, however, since the frequency of buses and trams decreases at night.

 Cost and time? The cost of outdoor movies varies from FREE to about €8/person. Reservations are generally recommended or required because space is often limited.

Laura Nicotra

Kids? Depending on how late your kids stay up, some of the programming may be suitable for younger audiences.

 Guide? No

When? Some of the venues show movies every night during the summer, while others may show films only once per week.

FUN FACTS

＊ Sometimes the outdoor cinema experience is enhanced when the director or an actor show up to discuss their work.

＊ The Austrian Forum of Culture in Rome hosts movies in the garden of their institute every summer.

Enrichment: Italy has a rich cinematic history known for neorealism, spaghetti westerns, Roberto Rossellini, Federico Fellini, Anna Magnani, Marcello Mastroianni, Sophia Loren, Ennio Morricone, Roberto Benigni, and more. There are so many important Italian movies to see, but start with Rome Open City *(1945),* Bicycle Thieves *(1948),* 8½ *(1963), and* La Grande Bellezza *(2013). You can also tour Cinecittà Studios, where many of these movies were made.*

www.casadelcinema.it

www.isoladelcinema.com

www.floatingtheatre.it

www.facebook.com/CINECITTAFILMFESTIVAL/

www.ilcinemainpiazza.it

www.arenagarbatella.it

www.facebook.com/Cinema-Tiziano-sito-ufficiale-159721814065333/

www.ferrerocinemas.com/adriano/index.php

www.sacherfilm.eu

www.austriacult.roma.it

Giardino dei Tarocchi

The Tarot Garden (*Il Giardino dei Tarocchi*) is an eccentric collection of modern sculpture based on Tarot cards. Created by artist Niki de Saint Phalle and a host of collaborators over a 24-year period (1974–1998), the two-hectare garden has 22 monumental figures made from reinforced concrete and covered with elaborate and brightly colored ceramic and glass mosaic. The tallest sculpture is 15 meters high! The garden was at least partly inspired by Antoni Gaudi's work in Barcelona, and the monster sculptures at *Sacro Bosco* in Bomarzo. The garden first opened to the public in 1998, though Saint Phalle continued to make design additions until her death in 2002.

Why go? There is really no other place on earth like *Il Giardino dei Tarocchi*, with its whimsically beautiful walkways through a magical and complex world. There is cascading water, a hanged man, a tree of life, and an apartment inside of the Empress. It is esoteric, challenging, and stunning — the apex of Saint Phalle's long career.

 Where? The Tarot Garden is just over 100 kilometers northwest of Rome, and less than 2 kilometers from the Lazio-Tuscany border. The best way to get there is by car.

 Cost and time? The entrance fee for the Tarot Garden is €12/adult. The site is not that large, so it will only take an hour or so.

 Kids? Absolutely! Kids will love going in and out of the colorful sculpture structures. It's FREE for kids under 7. There is no accommodation, however, for strollers or wheelchairs.

Guide? It was Saint Phalle's intention that there be no written description or audio guide for the various sculptures, so visitors are left with their own visceral interpretation of the garden.

 When? The Tarot Garden is open from April 1st to October 15th, and the first Saturday of each month from November to March. Check the opening times before you go.

FUN FACTS

* Tarot cards date back to 15th-century Italy, when they were used to play an assortment of games, much like regular playing cards today. It wasn't until the 18th century that the cards became an occultist tool for fortune telling, including the 22 trump cards called the *Major Arcana*, which inspired Saint Phalle to create her fabulous garden.
* Many sculptures by Saint Phalle are on display as public art around the world, from Jerusalem to San Diego.

Enrichment: *Other interesting and eclectic sites to the north of Rome include* La Scarzuola *and* Castello di Sammezzano. *The first is an "ideal city" designed by Tomaso Buzzi from 1958 to 1978 and realized by his nephew Marco Solari, who still lives in the beautifully complicated complex of buildings and theaters. It is about 20 kilometers north of Orvieto and open to the public with prior reservations (€10/person). The second is an abandoned castle that was redesigned in the mid-19th century in an elaborately stunning style reminiscent of India. It served as a hotel after WWII until the 1980s and has since sat vacant waiting for an investor to restore it anew. It is in the hills about 20 kilometers southeast of Florence and currently not open to the public.*

www.ilgiardinodeitarocchi.it/en/

www.lascarzuola.it/en/

www.sammezzano.info

Music

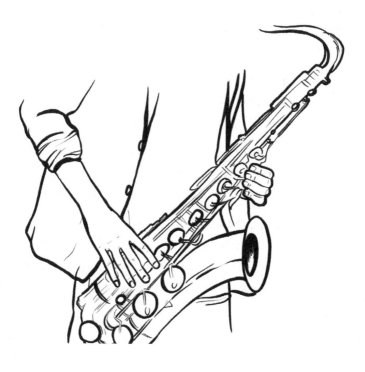

Opera at Caracalla

Since 1937, the Rome Opera House (*Teatro dell'Opera di Roma*) has held a summer season outside with the ruins of the Baths of Caracalla (*Terme di Caracalla*) as a backdrop. A huge temporary stage and tiered reserved seating structure for 4,000+ people are built every summer. The season includes opera, ballet, orchestral concerts, and other live music events. Each season is different!

Why go? This is a spectacular place to see a show. Warm summer evenings, an Aperol spritz from the adjacent bar, world-class music, in an amazing setting . . . what's not to love?

 Where? The *Terme di Caracalla* is 2 kilometers south-southeast from *Piazza Venezia*. The closest subway is the *Circo Massimo* stop on the B Line, and then a 600-meter walk.

 Cost and time? The shows are typically priced individually and not cheap, but well worth the experience, regardless of whether you are an opera fan. The shows usually last a couple of hours.

 Kids? A ballet or opera might hold the attention of younger kids, since there is lots of activity on stage, but the cost could be prohibitive if you're on the fence about going. If you do invest, share the plotline with the kids before the event.

 Guide? Of course, the operas will be in Italian. But there is often a simultaneous written translation into English on a screen near the stage. Even if you don't have kids coming along, reading up on the plotline beforehand is a good idea.

 When? The summer season typically goes from June to the beginning of August. It can get chilly at night so bring something light to cover up.

FUN FACTS

* In the summers of 2020 and 2021, the theater held outdoor shows in Circus Maximus (*Circo Massimo*) to allow for easier social distancing. It is unknown if the theater will continue with this venue in the future.
* Puccini's *Tosca* is a much sought-after ticket for the Caracalla season, partly because it is set at three locations in Rome: the Church of *Sant'Andrea della Valle*, *Palazzo Farnese*, and *Castel Sant'Angelo*.

Enrichment: Teatro dell'Opera di Roma *also has their traditional winter season in their primary theater on* Via del Viminale, *which has a stunning interior ringed with layers of semi-private box seats. There are many other opportunities to hear opera in Rome, including at the Auditorium and with Roma Opera Omnia.*

≡ www.operaroma.it/en/

La Casa del Jazz

Villa Osio was built in the 1930s just outside the Aurelian Walls by Arturo Osio, a wealthy Italian banker. After he died in 1968, the villa eventually fell into the hands of a known mafia boss, Enrico Nicoletti. As partial punishment for his crimes, the City of Rome confiscated the villa in 2001. In 2005, *Villa Osio* was opened to the public as *La Casa del Jazz* (The House of Jazz).

The goal of The House of Jazz is to encourage and promote jazz in Italy by providing a place where musicians, producers, critics, and laypeople can come together to explore the music. It has both indoor and outdoor theaters that host both Italian and international acts, a library and music archive, a recording studio, and a restaurant and bar. The outdoor space hosts summer shows, while the 150-seat indoor theater hosts winter performances, lectures, and film screenings. The rest of the 2.5-hectare grounds serve as a city park.

Fondazione Musica per Roma/Musacchio-Ianniello-Pasqualini

Why go? If you like jazz, there is no better place to see live music in the summertime than *La Casa del Jazz*. The outdoor setting under the umbrella pines and sparkling stars is fantastic. It's basically folding chairs on a dry lawn, but there is no bad seat. And the nearby Bo.Bo Bistro is an excellent place to start the evening.

 Where? *La Casa del Jazz* is 2.6 kilometers southeast of *Piazza Venezia,* about 100 meters from *Via Cristoforo Colombo*. The closest subway stop is Piramide on the B Line.

 Cost and time? The ticket cost for the show depends on the act of the evening. If you start with dinner at the bistro, this adventure could take all night!

 Kids? It depends on the show. An afternoon performance could be family friendly, but an evening show might have more of an outdoor nightclub vibe. *La Casa del Jazz* also does outreach to school kids with music classes.

 Guide? Not needed.

 When? Winter music shows inside are a cozy way to spend an evening, but *La Casa del Jazz* really shines on summer evenings. Check their performance schedule online to pick the best show for you.

FUN FACTS

＊ Apparently, Enrico Nicoletti was a moneyman for *La Banda della Magliana,* a mafia organization that has been active in Rome since the mid-1970s. They have been involved in the usual organized crime activities such as drug dealing, gambling, and money laundering, but what has set them apart are their ties to far-right politics and their tendency toward brutal violence.

* There is a plaque at the front gate to remember the victims of the mafia.
* Nicoletti enjoyed the high life, including *Villa Osio*, and was in and out of prison throughout his life. He died at age 84 in 2020, as the mafia web continues to untangle.

Enrichment: There are many other venues to listen to live jazz music in Rome, with names like The Cotton Club, The Elegance Café, Big Mama, and Alexanderplatz. There is even TramJazz, a refurbished tram car that plies the evening city tracks while patrons enjoy a candlelit dinner and listen to live jazz.

~ www.casadeljazz.com
~ www.bobobistrot.it

ADVENTURE #LXV

Auditorium Parco della Musica

The *Auditorium Parco della Musica*, recently renamed after famed Italian composer Ennio Morricone, is a complex of five concert venues of various sizes, including an outdoor theater. The theaters host hundreds of events annually including symphonies, dance, plays, jazz, rock, and cinema. Designed by Renzo Piano and inaugurated in 2002, the three primary indoor music halls, named Santa Cecilia, Sinopoli, and Petrassi, are reminiscent of scarab beetles and seat approximately 2,800, 1,200, and 700 people, respectively. The outdoor theater, called *La Cavea*, has seats for about 2,700 people and is active mostly in the summer. There is a smaller theater with a 300-person capacity. Also on site is a recording studio, rehearsal rooms, a restaurant and bar, and a bookstore.

Why go? There is so much entertainment going on at the Auditorium that eventually you will be drawn to it to see something special. The various sizes of performance spaces provide versatility to present almost any kind of show, from internationally famous touring acts to recitals of local performers, and from classical ballets to Elvis Costello. The architecture is also uniquely iconic and inspirational, and you can witness the way modern Romans go to see shows.

 Where? The Auditorium is 4 kilometers north of *Piazza Venezia*. The 2 tram from *Piazzale Flaminio* passes about 400 meters west of the theaters.

 Cost and time? The time and the cost of a visit to the Auditorium are completely dependent on what you are going to see.

Kids? There are many shows at the Auditorium that are specifically geared toward children. Check the calendar on their website to see what's coming. At Christmas time there is a small outdoor skating rink in front of the theater complex often in association with a small holiday craft market.

 Guide? Behind-the-scenes tours with Auditorium guides happen on weekends and holidays, and on weekdays with prior reservations. English tours occur at 12:30 and 2:30. They take about an hour.

 When? Whenever your favorite performers are scheduled to appear.

FUN FACTS

* During the construction of the Auditorium, an ancient Roman villa was unearthed that interfered with the original theater designs. After a year of modifications, the ruins were incorporated into a redesign and can be viewed between the theater structures in their own archeological museum, which is FREE.
* The Auditorium hosts the Rome Film Fest every October.

Enrichment: The primary opera, concert, and ballet theater in Rome is the Teatro dell'Opera di Roma. *It is active all year long, including producing the outdoor shows at* Terme di Caracalla. *There are dozens of beautiful theaters throughout Rome presenting a variety of plays, dance, and music. Some are quite grand, while others are quite modest. Rarely is anything in English, but opera, dance, and music have their own international language. A contemporary architecture tour of the neighborhood around the* Auditorium Parco della Musica *could include MAXXI and The Great Mosque.*

≡ www.auditorium.com

Oratorio del Gonfalone

The Confraternity of the Gonfalone was a prestigious group of lay Christian men, founded in the 13th century AD that supported the Catholic Church by carrying banners, or *gonfalone* in Italian, during periodic white-robed religious processions. They also conducted charity work that included aiding former prisoners and freeing Christian enslaved people. As they gained in popularity, Cardinal Alessandro Farnese helped build this beautifully ornate temple (or oratory) in the mid-16th century, complete with 12 large frescoed scenes depicting the Passion of Christ (i.e., the end of the life of Jesus) and a carved wooden ceiling. The brotherhood was eventually dissolved in 1890 and the *Oratorio del Gonfalone* was confiscated by the Italian Government.

Since 1960, the Oratory has been entrusted to the Roman Polyphonic Choir, which specializes in Renaissance music and produces an annual series of soloist and chamber recitals in the space. The frescoes were restored to their original luster in 2000.

Why go? The Oratory has been called the Mannerist Sistine Chapel, having been painted in the late Renaissance, a few decades after the Sistine. The Oratory artists were masters of their day, but none rose to the fame of Michelangelo. Today, it is a uniquely complete period room, with the floors, walls, and ceiling all preserved as they were when the Oratory was finished. To listen to live Renaissance music in this venue is truly a special opportunity.

 Where? The *Oratorio del Gonfalone* is less than 1.5 kilometers west of *Piazza Venezia*, not far from the Tiber River. Take any bus that goes up *Corso Vittorio Emanuele II*.

Cost and time? The cost and time depend on the show, but it should be in the range of €15-25/person.

 Kids? Not really, unless they like classical music.

 Guide? There are tours of the Oratory on Saturday mornings that discuss the history of the art in the grand room and end with a couple of chamber music pieces. Check the website for details. Tours can be arranged any day with a private guide.

 When? The music shows at the Oratory are usually only once per week during their season. The best time to go is whenever there is a musical program that appeals to you. The room is so beautiful that it almost doesn't matter.

FUN FACTS

✳ The *Oratorio del Gonfalone* was always in private ownership and funded by wealthy patrons.

✳ Becoming a member of the Confraternity of the Gonfalone was a prestigious achievement.

✳ Mannerism is the period between the great artists of the High Renaissance — such as da Vinci, Raphael, and Michelangelo — and the Caravaggio revolution.

~~~~~~

Enrichment: *Just a few blocks from the Oratory is another privately held church called* Sant'Eligio degli Orefici. *It was built in the 16th century AD for the Guild of Goldsmiths, an organization that has since evolved into the University of Goldsmiths. Raphael initially designed the church and it is the only one in Rome, except Saint Peter's Basilica, at least partially attributed to him. The church is typically closed to the public but allows visitors by special arrangement (ask your guide for help).*

≡ www.oratoriogonfalone.eu/home-english/

ADVENTURE #LXVII

Roma Opera Omnia

Roma Opera Omnia is a group of professional art historians, singers, and musicians who combine short tours of beautiful historic places in Rome with the performance of live Renaissance and Baroque music on traditional and ancient instruments. Their regular public presentations have taken place at various locations around the city, including *Palazzo Doria Pamphilj*, the Church Sant'Agnese in Agone, *Palazzo Barberini*, and *Villa Farnesina*.

Why go? The association of specialists with expertise in a variety of fields provides a unique experience that melds the history of a place with the music of the period. Often the tours and concerts are conducted and performed after hours once the tourists have left and provide for a distinctive adventure. Some performances are even combined with dinner or *aperitivo*, sometimes on a rooftop deck or in a palace dining room. It makes for an amazing evening!

 Where? The various locations where *Roma Opera Omnia* tour and perform are generally in central Rome and are reachable via public transportation.

 Cost and time? The prices vary depending on the program but start around €20/person. The tours generally last about an hour, followed by a one-hour concert.

 Kids? Not really, unless your tween or teen is in the school band or orchestra, which might make it a particularly fun event for them.

 Guide? *Roma Opera Omnia* programs start with a guided tour of the specific location, be it a palace or church.

 When? Their programs regularly repeat so you can choose a time, cost, and location that is most convenient to you.

FUN FACTS

* The Roman School of composers in the 16th and 17th centuries produced polyphonic music primarily for the church.
* Polyphony is a type of music with two or more simultaneous lines of independent melody.
* One of the programs that *Roma Opera Omnia* performs features Gregorian chants in the Church of *Santa Maria della Concezione dei Cappuccini* and is set above the Capuchin Crypt, which houses the

bones of deceased monks. It may be the perfect Halloween experience. The church and crypt are located near *Piazza Barberini.*

Enrichment: *There is also a National Museum of Musical Instruments near* Porta Maggiore *in Rome. It is located inside* Palazzina Samoggia, *which is on* Piazza Santa Croce in Gerusalemme. *The museum collection includes over 3,000 instruments accumulated by opera singer Evan Gorga (1865–1957). The museum opened in 1974 and has instruments spanning over 2,000 years. The* Auditorium Parco della Musica *also has an instrument museum, which is FREE and open from October to June (closed on Thursdays).*

www.romaoperaomnia.com

www.museostrumentimusicali.beniculturali.it

www.santacecilia.it/en/auditorium/museo-degli-strumenti-musicali/

Roma Opera Omnia

Terrestrial Adventures

Hill Towns

Frascati

Looking southeast from Rome, the Alban Hills are readily apparent as they rise above the horizon. Originally a volcano, for centuries the hills have attracted Roman elite for their summertime fresh air, cooler elevation, and country views. The smattering of wealthy 16th and 17th century castles across the landscape became known as the *Castelli Romani* (Roman Castles). At the center of the *Castelli Romani* is the town of Frascati, which is also known for the white wines grown in the surrounding volcanic soils. Following a major rebuild of the town after WWII, Frascati remains a destination for Romans.

Why go? Frascati is a quaint little town with over a dozen villas in the countryside. Many are closed to the public, but some have scheduled private tours (*Villa Falconieri*, *Mondragone*, and *Parisi*), have open public gardens (*Villa Torlonia* and *Sciarra*), or have been turned into hotels (*Villa Grazioli*, *Tuscolana*, and *Vecchia*). They provide a great excuse to go walking in the hills on a nice day.

Frascati is also a place for wine and food. There are tours of local vineyards and wine-tastings in local cafés. *Porchetta* (roast pork) sandwiches are a local specialty, especially in the shops around the *Piazza del Mercato*. And don't forget the *Pupazza Frascatana*, a sweet cookie with a graphic depiction of a three-breasted woman — two are for milk and one is for wine!

 Where? Frascati is only 19 kilometers southeast of Rome. Of course it's possible to drive (50 minutes from Centro), but the *Castelli Romani* train leaves Rome-Termini for Frascati every hour (€2/person) and takes only 30 minutes.

 Cost and time? Many of these things will cost money, but it depends on your ambitions. Frascati is most often a day trip from Rome.

 Kids? Teens and tween will like the train, villa history, and walk in the countryside. Smaller kids will be challenged. It's a short uphill walk from the train station into the main town.

 Guide? Learning about the details of the villas or winemaking will be better with a guide, but you don't need a guide to enjoy your time in Frascati.

 When? It depends. If you're going to walk in the hills and vineyards, a nice weather day is the most appropriate. But if you're going for the food and wine, or to just walk around town, any day is a good day.

FUN FACTS

✳ The Rome to Frascati train is one of the oldest in Italy, opening in 1856.

✳ The view of *Villa Aldobrandini* (available to host parties) from the promenade above the train station is spectacular.

✳ *Villa Falconieri* has some fantastic murals. One room is entirely covered with lush green frescoes that almost make it feel like being outside in the garden.

✳ Frascati celebrates *Carnevale* for a week in February with costumes and parades. All the kids will love the parade!

Enrichment: *Ariccia, another* Castelli Romani *town in this book, is perhaps the most famous town for porchetta. There is a grape festival at the beginning of October every year in the nearby town of Marino. It's possible to hike to the ancient Roman ruins of Tusculum from Frascati, which is roughly 10 kilometers roundtrip. The Abbey of San Nilo, in the nearby* Castelli Romani *town of Grottaferrata, is also worth a visit.*

www.minardifrascatiwinery.com
www.stradadeivinideicastelliromani.it

Tivoli

Tivoli is a hill town east of Rome located above beautiful waterfalls on the Aniene River, which eventually flows into the Tiber River in northern Rome. Tracing its origins back to the 13th century BC, there are still two ancient Roman temples overlooking the falls devoted to pre-Christian deities. Eventually, Tivoli became one of the places where the Roman elite built their country villas and castles, from Emperor Hadrian (2nd century AD) to Pope Pius II (15th century AD) to Cardinal Ippolito d'Este (16th century AD).

Why go? The three main reasons to visit Tivoli are the *Parco Villa Gregoriana*, *Villa d'Este*, and Hadrian's Villa (the latter two have their own adventures in this book). *Parco Villa Gregoriana* encompasses the forested river gorge below the Temples of Vesta and Sybil. The park has a system of winding walking trails that lead to ancient sites, caves, and waterfall overlooks. In the village, there are also the remains of a 2nd century AD amphitheater (*Anfiteatro di Bleso*) and *Rocca Pia*, a fortress built by Pope Pius II to control the region. It has only recently been opened to the public.

 Where? The Tivoli train station is 28 kilometers east-northeast from central Rome. A train leaves Rome-Termini for Tivoli almost every hour (starting at €3/person). A bus goes from the Tivoli train station to *Villa Gregoriana*, *Villa d'Este*, and Hadrian's Villa for €1.30/person. It also takes less than an hour to drive from Rome to Tivoli.

 Cost and time? *Parco Villa Gregoriana* costs €8/person, and the walk will take an hour or so. The amphitheater and *Rocca Pia* are currently FREE, but check the website for pricing changes. A visit to the park, the old town center, and *Villa d'Este* would make a nice day trip from Rome.

Creative Commons Adrian Pingston (Arpingstone)

 Kids? Children will love to wander through the medieval village of Tivoli. Watch the little kids in the *Parco Villa Gregoriana,* however, because it is after all a gorge.

 Guide? A FREE guide may greet you when you arrive to *Rocca Pia,* but one is probably not needed for the park.

 When? Nice days, since much of this adventure is outdoors. Bring water to your exploration of *Parco Villa Gregoriana* when it is hot. The park is closed from the middle of December until the end of February.

FUN FACTS

* The stone used to build many of the regal buildings in ancient Rome came from the travertine quarries of Tivoli and the nearby town of Guidonia.
* It is likely that the stones used to build the amphitheater were repurposed in the construction of *Rocca Pia* 1,300 years later.
* *Rocco Pia* served as a prison until 1960.

✳ *Terme Di Roma* is a commercial thermal spa in *Bagni di Tivoli* known for its *aquae albule*, or white sulphurous water. Emperor Hadrian was thought to use the water to feed some of the numerous pools at his nearby villa. Today the spa facility encompasses four large pools and all the modern conveniences, including a hotel, restaurants, and various wellness treatments.

~~~~~~~~~~~

Enrichment: *Obviously, the main reasons to go to Tivoli are Villa d'Este and Hadrian's Villa, which should not be missed. The Subiaco Monastery is 40 kilometers farther east from Tivoli.*

☰ www.fondoambiente.it/parco-villa-gregoriana-eng/

ADVENTURE #LXX

Orvieto

Orvieto is a beautiful hilltop village in southwest Umbria. Settled for over 2,500 years because of the protection afforded by its high perch above precipitous walls, it has been valued by Etruscans, Romans, and Popes. Today, Orvieto is primarily a tourist town, drawing people to see the black and white stripes of the amazing cathedral, walk the alleyways of town, and drink wine from the local vineyards.

Why go? Orvieto makes for a great excursion from Rome either for a long day or a weekend. It has history, beauty, food, and friendly Italians.

 Where? Orvieto is 96 kilometers north of Rome. It takes about the same length of time to drive as it does to take the train (starting at about €8/person): about 90 minutes. Across the street from the Orvieto train station is a funicular that transports people from the valley up to the town (€2.60/person for a return trip). The upper funicular station is located at the eastern end of the village.

 Cost and time? Your cost and time will depend on your objectives. At the very least, it will take a full day to see Orvieto starting in Rome, but it is also a nice place to spend a full weekend.

 Kids? Kids will love the train and the funicular rides. Walking the quaint streets of Orvieto will keep them engaged only until the next gelato. But just wait until they discover the over 1,200 excavated grottoes under the town. For millennia, the people of Orvieto have been digging to make more room, for security, and to find water. There is an hour-long tour to take you down into the grottoes (€7/adult).

Guide? There is much to discover about Orvieto. A local Umbrian guide would love to show you around.

When? Whenever you want to escape the hubbub of Rome!

FUN FACTS

* So the story goes, in 1263 a piece of communion bread bled onto a cloth in the town of Bolsena. The Orvieto Cathedral is now home to this Eucharist miracle relic, which is celebrated by Catholics on Corpus Domini, a feast that occurs 60 days after Easter.

* The Well of Saint Patrick (*Pozzo di San Patrizio*) was built in Orvieto during the early 1500s to provide a safe water supply in case the town was under siege by invaders. The well consists of two intertwined spiral ramps: one for mules to descend 53 meters to the groundwater and the other for mules to ascend fully loaded with containers of water. It will cost you €5 to recreate the 248-step journey. Windows into the interior open cylinder of the well are very photogenic.

Enrichment: There are many adventures in this book that are on the way to and from Orvieto from Rome. Civita di Bagnoregio, Lago di Bolsena, Montefiascone, and Bosco del Sasseto can all be visited from Orvieto on a long weekend.

www.assoguide.it

www.orvietounderground.it/index.php/en/

196

Civita di Bagnoregio

This is probably the most photogenic village-on-a-hill in all of Italy. Sitting atop a rocky plateau and dating back to Etruscan times more than 2,500 years ago, *Civita di Bagnoregio* is tiny, with only a few dozen buildings in constant gravitational threat of crumbling into the surrounding valley. Indeed, it is so small that the full-time population is reported to be only about dozen people. Its popularity with tourists, however, is keeping it going as there are several restaurants and lodging opportunities. A 300-meter footbridge, reconstructed in 2013, links the village to the nearby town of Bagnoregio, and the toll charged to tourists to park and climb to the village is a local goldmine.

Why go? This village is beautiful from the moment you see it, along the entire footbridge, and when you're wandering through the few tiny alleyways inside. Yes, tour buses stop here regularly on their way from Rome to points north, but they don't stop for long — a couple photos and a gelato and they're off again. Don't let them stop you from getting your pictures too, especially considering the impermanence of these settlements.

 Where? *Civita di Bagnoregio* is about 90 kilometers north of Rome. The easiest way to get there is by car, which will normally take less than two hours. However, taking a train to Orvieto and then a bus to Bagnoregio is possible. The *Comune* (municipality) runs a shuttle from the parking lot and along the footbridge for those that need it.

 Cost and time? The toll for the footbridge is €5/person. The approach is mostly uphill and you have to stop periodically to catch your breath and take another picture. The village doesn't

take much time to see, but you'll probably stop for a drink or gelato before you head back downhill. It probably won't take more than couple of hours, even if you stay for dinner.

 Kids? The place is storybook beautiful so most kids will love this adventure. The littlest kids may need some help getting up and down the footbridge, but it's a pretty cool experience.

Guide? There are undoubtedly some stories of the village that are best told by a guide. Like why did the Etruscans want to live on this rock in the first place?

When? The popularity of the village has necessitated implementing summer hours (unless you're staying overnight or have restaurant reservations): from 8 am to 8 pm on weekends and holidays and from 9 am to 8 pm on weekdays. The footbridge may be FREE in the off-season, when the ticket booth is often closed.

FUN FACTS

* Now that the village has been discovered by the tourist industry, there is a more active attempt to limit the erosion and potential impacts of earthquakes that have caused the place to shrink over the centuries.
* There is a small geology museum just inside the village walls that offers information about the history and science of the landslides that formed the town.
* There is a tunnel out the back end of the village that historically provided access to the valley below, but it is no longer in use.

Enrichment: Other towns on the top of hills near Bagnoregio include Orvieto and Montefiascone. Lago di Bolsena and Sacro Bosco in Bomarzo are also adventures in this book that could be combined with a visit to Bagnoregio.

www.civitadibagnoregio.cloud

www.museogeologicoedellefrane.it/en/index.html

Calcata

Calcata is a small and picturesque hilltop village that overlooks the Treja River valley and dates back to the 14th century AD. The pedestrian alleyways of the medieval-walled town are accessed through a single main gate. In the 1930s, fearing that the buildings of Calcata would collapse in an earthquake, the town was condemned and the people were moved to the newly established town of Calcata Nuova on nearby safer ground. By the 1970s, many squatters had moved into the abandoned old village, which quickly evolved into a kind of new-age artisan and craftsman colony. The government reversed the condemnation order in the 1990s, and many of the squatters eventually purchased their homes and studios. Today, the town continues to support an artistic community and welcomes outsiders to their art galleries and workshops.

Why go? Calcata is fascinating in its mix of medieval architecture and modern creative sensibilities. It is an opportunity to support the entrepreneurial spirit of local artists and craftsmen in their own workshops. In addition to the many shops displaying handmade arts and crafts, there are also a few bistros and lodging options. All of this makes for an excellent opportunity to get out of the city for a stroll into something new.

 Where? Calcata is 36 kilometers north of central Rome and it takes about an hour to drive there. A parking lot for *Calcata Vecchia* is located about 500 meters east of the gate in *Calcata Nuova*. It is also possible to get to Calcata via train and bus, which takes at least two hours.

 Cost and time? Walking around the old village is FREE and will take an hour or so. Buying some art or crafts, of course, is up to you.

 Kids? Yes, the artistic community is very welcoming of children, and the kids will also enjoy exploring the old village.

 Guide? Not needed. Seeing the town on your own is easy and fun.

When? There is more activity, both from the artistic residents and visitors, in the summertime. In the winter, the alleyways of town can be quite quiet.

FUN FACTS

✳ In the Middle Ages, when religious relics were all the rage, perhaps over a dozen churches throughout Europe claimed to have the foreskin of Jesus, also called the Holy Prepuce. Of course, at least one of these found its way to Rome, where it was stolen by a German soldier during the sacking of 1527. During his retreat, the soldier left the foreskin in Calcata, where it was annually paraded through the streets on the Feast of the Circumcision (January 1st). In 1983, the ancient prepuce was stolen from the custody of the local priest, and the quest for the holy foreskin continues!

✳ The current population of *Calcata Vecchia* is about 150 people.

Enrichment: The Treja Valley Regional Park, just below Calcata, protects 658 hectares of forest and 13 kilometers of the Treja River, which is a tributary of the Tiber. This includes the Cascate di Monte Gelato, which is indeed a pretty waterfall. Disappointingly, there is no mountain of ice cream (gelato simply means ice cold). Hiking on the beautiful trails of the park is an excellent morning adventure before heading for Calcata in the afternoon. Adjacent to the park and just to the north of Calcata, is the Opera Bosco Museum of Art in Nature. It was inaugurated in 1996 by Anne Demijttenaere, who continues to create fascinatingly beautiful art installations in the forest made only from natural material in celebration of impermanence. Distinguishing between art and nature is a challenge! The outdoor museum trails can be steep, so come ready for a hike.

www.calcata.info

www.operabosco.eu

Food & Wine

Neighborhood Food Markets

Almost every neighborhood in Rome has a local farmers market where there are individual vendors selling nearly everything people need on a daily basis. In a typical market there will be stalls selling pasta, cheese, fruit, vegetables, meat, fish, wine, olive oil, and spices. There may even be people selling baking supplies, dinner plates, and cleaning products. The markets themselves can be in a large hall under a common roof or the vendors may have separate open-air stalls. Neighborhood markets are part of many people's daily routine in Rome and are typically most active in the morning. There are literally dozens of markets throughout the city. The best known include Testaccio, Esquilino, *Piazza dell'Unità*, *Piazza San Cosimato*, and *Campo de'Fiori*.

All the markets have unique characteristics. Some have food stalls that sell sandwiches and quick meals; some have vendors that sell clothes; and others even have evening musical entertainment targeting the local community. For the purest form of the food market (i.e., no limoncello in phallic-shaped bottles), you may have to venture from the tourist areas.

Why go? If you want to see how local Romans go about their regular lives, or maybe you just need a piece of fresh fruit, the neighborhood markets are the place to be. Most of the products will be locally produced in the Lazio region, and many of them are also organic (or BIO). Going to the market has been part of the Roman lifestyle for millennia.

 Where? No matter where you are in Rome you won't be more than a few blocks from a local market.

 Cost and time? Strolling through a market is FREE of course, but how much you buy there is up to you.

 Kids? Yes, not only will the kids experience purchasing food closer to the source, they will see that food production entails an entire community of people living together. They can also see what foods are in season, and maybe get to try something new. Let the kids select and buy food for a picnic or collect the ingredients for your dinner meal.

Guide? Not really, unless you are interested in knowing more about local foods, how they are produced, and how they get to the consumer.

When? Most neighborhood markets are open early in the day and close down by the early afternoon. They are typically open six days per week (closed on Sundays).

~~~~~~

FUN FACTS

* Tomatoes originated in South America and first made it to Italy around 1548. There are over 300 varieties currently grown here.
* Italians think so highly of the diversity of their mozzarella that they typically consider it a separate food group from other cheeses. Definitely search out the *mozzarella di bufala*, typically made in the region of Campania from the milk of water buffalo.

~~~~~~

Enrichment: With so many kinds of tomatoes and mozzarella in Rome, it might be fun to have a caprese salad taste test with the various kinds of each. Artichokes also hold a unique position in Roman cooking, and there are several traditional ways of preparing them that you could try. And if cooking is your thing, there are all sorts of classes around town that specialize in teaching how to cook the Roman culinary mainstays.

☰ www.marketsofrome.com/food-market

SAID dal 1923

SAID dal 1923 is a chocolate factory, shop, and restaurant. Originally opened in Rome in 1923 with a Swiss partner under the name of "Zurich," the fascist Italian government forced the company to change its name to *Società Anonima Industria Dolciumi* (SAID), meaning "Confectionery Industry Anonymous Company." Not very sexy, but it has stuck. The original factory in the San Lorenzo neighborhood was bombed in 1943 by the Allies, but the company soon reopened in its current location.

In 2006, the grandson of the founder diversified the company from a chocolate factory to include a chocolate shop and a restaurant that specializes in chocolate pastries and drinks. They serve traditional foods as well, but it's hard to get past chocolate, since the smell is in the air. Unfortunately, other than the chocolate molds that line the walls of the restaurant, there really isn't a public window into the chocolate production side of the business. SAID has also opened stores in London and Dubai.

Why go? If you like chocolate, there is something very special about being served a hot chocolate in a chocolate cup on a chocolate saucer with a

chocolate spoon. You can choose which flavor of chocolate (e.g., dark, milk, white) you'd like. If you like chocolate, nothing else really needs to be said (pun intended).

 Where? *SAID dal 1923* is less than 3 kilometers east of *Piazza Venezia*. The closest subway stop is Vittorio Emanuele on the A Line, which is still about a kilometer away.

 Cost and time? The chocolate items on the SAID menu are understandably priced, given their high quality. A fantastic hot chocolate, for instance, will cost about €6. The other menu items are typically priced. The cozy atmosphere, including armchairs and couches, is worth the visit.

 Kids? Yes, absolutely! But maybe not right before bedtime. Plan some high-energy activities to follow this adventure.

 Guide? Not needed.

 When? If you're just going for a chocolate fix, getting a seat during the off-peak hours for a chocolate "tea" or *aperitivo* is relatively easy. If you're going for dinner, it might be good to make a reservation.

FUN FACTS

* Chocolate first made it to Italy from the Americas in the early 1600s, and it was originally treated as medicinal (maybe one of the reasons why monk-made chocolate can still be found in abbey shops that specialize in medicines). It wasn't long before it was being infused with lemon and jasmine to vary the flavor. Eventually, chocolate made it into many Italian recipes, not just desserts.

* In 1678, the king of Italy licensed a Turinese merchant to make a chocolate drink with layers of cream and coffee, which is still popular there today.

Enrichment: *The San Lorenzo neighborhood has long been associated with the working class and the communist party and is worth a walk around. Over 3,000 people died there during the bombing on July 19, 1943. The neighborhood is now heavily influenced by the students from nearby* La Sapienza University, *with lively bars and an active street art community.*

≡ www.said.it/en/

ADVENTURE #LXXV

Ariccia

Ariccia is a village in the *Castelli Romani*, south of Rome, that has a settlement history back to the 8th to 9th century BC. There is obviously a lot to know about the place, but what brings us on this adventure is the porchetta. *La porchetta di Ariccia* is a famous pork roast seasoned with rosemary, black pepper, fennel, and garlic. Crispy (!) on the outside, white and marbled on the inside, the aroma is how I wish my grandmother's kitchen smelled. Slices of porchetta can be accompanied with potatoes and vegetables or layered on a fresh roll for an amazing sandwich. Recipes have been passed through generations of Ariccian families, and though porchetta can be found in other parts of Italy, it is the best in Ariccia.

In 1950, the mayor of Ariccia started a porchetta festival celebrating what had been recognized as the town's unique culinary contributions. It has grown since then to include countless restaurants and booths that are concentrated under the smaller bridge along *Via Borgo San Rocco*, and along *Via dell'Uccelliera*. On weekend afternoons most of the tables fill with urban Romans getting out of town for a fantastic lunch.

Why go? To eat porchetta, of course! Ariccia has also become known for their *fraschette*, which is a kind of wine tavern. The *Castelli Romani* is a vital wine-producing area, and originally the fraschette proprietors would

serve their own wine and not much food. But with the popularity of porchetta, the fraschette have evolved to serve this delicacy too. You will have to go to Ariccia many times to figure out which *fraschetta* is your favorite.

 Where? A *panino con la porchetta* (porchetta sandwich) in Ariccia is only 25 kilometers from central Rome, and it will take less than an hour to drive there. The train from Rome-Termini ends at the Albano Laziale station, which is still shy of Ariccia by 1.5 kilometers (walk or taxi is possible). The train/taxi trip takes less than an hour and is the same train that goes by Castel Gandolfo, the Pope's summer residence.

 Cost and time? A visit to Ariccia for lunch will probably take a couple of hours. A porchetta sandwich costs about €4.

 Kids? *La Selvotta* is a porchetta restaurant just outside of town where all the rustic tables are outside under the trees. The park-like setting is perfect for kids who might be restless in a more traditional *fraschetta* tavern.

 Guide? No, unless they're hungry too!

When? The annual porchetta festival is still going strong in Ariccia and usually takes place during the first weekend of September.

FUN FACTS

* Porchetta is only made with pork from a female pig because they are leaner and tastier.
* The basic porchetta process is as follows: 1) debone a choice female pig, 2) apply only fresh spices like your grandma showed you, 3) tightly roll, but not too tight, into a log and tie, 4) cook in a very large oven for 3-4 hours, 5) jack up the heat for the last five minutes to make the outside skin crispy, 6) cool, 7) slice, 8) eat! Of course, there is more to it than that, but you get the idea.

Enrichment: *Before entering into Ariccia from Rome,* Via Appia Nuova *passes over a tall bridge that spans a short deep canyon. The original bridge built in 1854 was bombed by the Germans during their retreat in WWII. After the first rebuild crumbled, it had to be rebuilt yet again in 1967. It became known as the "suicide" bridge until protective netting was erected along its entire length. Upon entering Ariccia from the bridge, the road passes into Bernini's 17th-century* Piazza di Corte. *The round church on the right (*Santa Maria Assunta*) and the* Palazzo Chigi *on the left were both designed by Bernini and financed by the Chigi family (i.e., Pope Alexander VII). The* Palazzo *is open to the public (€8/adult, closed Mondays) and has beautiful baroque art (including the room of portraits of "beautiful women"), ornate apartments, and a large forested garden out back. There is also a quick sketch that Bernini left on one of the unfinished walls that has been preserved.*

www.laselvottadiariccia.it
www.palazzochigiariccia.it

Monti Cecubi Winery

Wine in ancient Rome was a daily necessity for almost everyone, both men and women, from aristocrats to peasants and enslaved people. But the wine they drank, apart from being produced from grapes, bears little resemblance to the wines of today. Their wine was fermented in terracotta pots, called amphora, that were lined with beeswax and buried to their necks in the ground. The alcohol in the resulting product (relatively low by today's standards) killed the bacteria in the liquid, making it healthier than the water of the day. It likely tasted quite awful, but they mixed it with fruit and honey to make it more palatable.

The Monti Cecubi Winery, located outside the town of Itri in southern Lazio, uses the same traditional indigenous varieties of grapes that were used by the ancient Romans. Fortunately, they are not faithful to ancient fermentation process, and use only organic methods to produce their wines. The end result is some fine-tasting wine.

Why go? Monti Cecubi makes nine varieties of wines from handpicked grapes. Tours of the vineyard allow you to see how the grapes are grown, how the wine is made, and try the final product.

 Where? The Monti Cecubi Winery is 110 kilometers southeast from central Rome. It will take over two hours to drive there. A train can get you nearby, but the winery is out in the country, so the last leg is more difficult. The winery is only 6 kilometers from Sperlonga.

 Cost and time? A tour of the vineyard and winery takes about two hours and costs €20/person. It includes tasting three wines and a sampling of snacks.

Kids? The kids might enjoy getting outside and seeing how to grow grapes, but they probably won't enjoy the wine that much.

 Guide? A local guide can facilitate tours to the winery in English and can meet your train in Sperlonga. These tours are €45/person.

 When? Tours of the winery are typically only by appointment from Thursday to Saturday or arranged through a guide.

FUN FACTS

* Monti Cecubi also makes olive oil. The olives are handpicked in October and November and milled within 12 hours of being picked. You can see the oil making process if you visit during those months.
* The hills around the winery are popular for mountain biking, and there is also a guided "hike and wine" tour.

Enrichment: *The ancient villa of Emperor Tiberius and the associated museum are literally on the beach at Sperlonga. An excellent seasonal weekend would combine the winery, the beach, and the villa. The* Castello di Itri, *from the 9th century AD, is also not far away from the winery.*

www.monticecubi.it

www.amyclaeexperience.com/the-old-roman-wine-tour

Amyclae Experience by Irene Chinappi

Montefiascone

Montefiascone is a town on a volcanic ridge that overlooks Lake Bolsena. The high vantage point provided a territorial advantage exploited by people from at least the 9th century BC. There were likely wood and stone fortifications on the site for millennia, especially after the Romans built *Via Cassia* close by. Friction between the Popes and the Holy Roman Emperors necessitated even greater security, resulting in *Rocca dei Papi*, an early 13th century fortress. Popes regularly visited the fort through the 14th century, when it gradually fell into disuse. The area has since suffered from plagues, earthquakes, and WWII bombings.

Throughout most of recorded history, however, Montefiascone has been primarily known for one thing: wine! The elevation, moderate climate, and old volcanic soils in the area grow some tasty grapes. In 1958, the town held its first wine festival, which is now an annual two-week party every August. The festival celebrates excellent wine that has achieved DOC status (*Denominazione di Origine Controllata*), which means it is produced locally and meets certain quality standards.

Why go? Go for the lake and the view, stay for the wine. Seriously, Lake Bolsena is an excellent place to cool off in the summertime, and an outdoor café in Montefiascone in the late afternoon is a great place to relax with a glass of the local wine. It has all the makings of a fantastic day!

 Where? Montefiascone is 80 kilometers north-northwest from central Rome. It takes about an hour and a half to drive there. A train also goes to Montefiascone in less than two hours, but the station is still a ten-minute taxi ride uphill to the town.

 Cost and time? Since the travel time for this excursion is at least several hours and includes wine, this adventure might be better attempted as an overnight. A bottle of wine will cost about €10, but how much you spend on the rest of the weekend is up to you.

 Kids? Visiting *Lago di Bolsena* in the summer is a very kid-friendly activity. Drinking wine, probably not so much.

 Guide? Not needed.

 When? The DOC wine is available year-round, but the wine festival is in August.

FUN FACTS

✳ Legend has it that in 1111, a German bishop was heading to Rome for the coronation of the Holy Roman Emperor. He sent his aide ahead to identify taverns along the way that had good wine. The aide was to mark a tavern with the word "est", or "it is" in Latin, meaning that good

Amyclae Experience by Irene Chinappi

wine could be found within. When the bishop got to Montefiascone, he found the words "Est! Est!! Est!!!" over the door of a tavern. He agreed so much with the aide's review of the wine that he returned after the coronation and drank himself to death.

* The Montefiascone wine festival includes a drumming procession in period costume that is dedicated to the bishop.
* Gioachino Rossini set his 1817 operatic version of Cinderella, with an evil stepfather instead of an evil stepmother, in Montefiascone.
* Montefiascone hosts an annual film festival in July, which showcases new Italian directors.

Enrichment: There are also some beautiful churches in Montefiascone. San Flaviano has unique architecture for a 13th century church, with creepy medieval frescoes of martyrdom, and is the final resting place of that alcoholic bishop. Wine pilgrims have been known to pour wine over his gravestone to commemorate his palate. The medieval fortress of Rocca dei Papi and museum are also open to the public (€5/person, but FREE for kids under 12). The fort was redesigned in the 16th century by Antonio Da Sangallo the Younger, who specialized in building fortresses for the popes.

montefiascone.artecitta.it

www.mytuscia.com/montefiascone.html

www.cantinaleonardi.it

www.estfilmfestival.it

Walking & Hiking

Parco di Veio

The Regional Park of Veio is nearly 15,000 hectares of rolling upland forestland and meadows cut by wooded stream gorges. The area, north of Rome, includes nine villages and agricultural lands that produce wine, olive oil, grains, and grazing for livestock. There are extensive hiking trails in the park through upland oak forests, along riparian corridors of alder, poplar, and willow, and occasionally across farmers' fields. The Cremera River, a tributary of the Tiber, and the Sorbo Valley are the landscape backbones of the park.

The park gets its name from the ancient Etruscan city of Veio, whose ruins are inside the park and just outside the village of Isola Farnese. Dating back as far as 9th to 11th centuries BC, the ruins of Veio include temples, a necropoli, and *Ponte Sodo*, a 70-meter long tunnel excavated through a hillside for flood control. There is also a waterfall (*Cascate della Mola*) adjacent to the primary archeological site.

Why go? If you are getting tired of the urbanization of Rome and need a quick nature fix, there is no better place to go than the *Parco di Veio*. It is very close to the city but provides unique exposure to the natural flora and fauna of Lazio. The park is by no means a wilderness experience, but it definitely allows for a back-to-nature escape. The hiking trails are varied and reasonably well marked, including flat walks though grasslands and wading through a stream (to access *Ponte Sodo*).

 Where? There are many access points to *Parco di Veio*, but the primary trailhead for the ruins of Veio is only 16 kilometers north-northwest of central Rome. It will take about half an hour to drive there. Taking a bus to Isola Farnese is possible, but it will take over an hour, require at least one transfer, and you'll still need to get a taxi to the trailhead.

 Cost and time? *Parco di Veio* is FREE. It is at least a half-day proposition to do a little hike in the park and/or see some of the ruins of Veio.

 Kids? Yes, getting out into nature is good for people of all ages. The Sorbo Valley, among other places in the park, is an excellent place for a picnic. You may even get to see the free-range cows and horses.

 Guide? If you want to know more about the ancient city of Veio, or if you are unsure of finding your way in an outdoor setting, a guide will be helpful. But if you are looking for a relaxing experience with nature, a guide is not necessary.

 When? When the weather is predictably good, especially summertime.

FUN FACTS

✳ The large-horned, semi-feral Maremmana cows that you might see in the Sorbo Valley is an ancient variety bred by the Etruscans. They are currently making a comeback in the region.

✳ After a long absence, wolves have also recently returned to *Parco di Veio*. They primarily prey on wild boar and are being monitored by park managers using remote motion-sensor cameras.

Enrichment: *The Etruscans of Veio were active water engineers. In addition to the flood-control tunnel, they constructed at least 50 kilometers of tunnels and aqueducts to move water where they wanted it. The fall of Veio to the Romans occurred around 396 BC after a ten-year siege, when the Romans breached the city walls via underground tunnels. If you want to learn more about the Etruscans and see some of the archeological artifacts from Veio, visit the National Etruscan Museum at* Villa Giulia *in Rome.*

☰ www.parcodiveio.it

ADVENTURE #LXXIX

Bosco del Sasseto di Torre Alfina

Old-growth forest is a rarity in Europe, where thousands of years of natural resource exploitation has impacted almost every square meter of land. That makes the 61 hectares of 300- to 400-year-old deciduous forest outside the tiny village of Torre Alfina in northern Lazio a unique and vital piece of a scarce primeval ecosystem. The *Bosco del Sasseto* has over 20 species of native trees including beech, elm, sycamore, and oak. They can grow as large as 25 meters tall and one meter in diameter. The rich biodiversity of

the understory includes ferns and mosses that are naturally integrated into the steep and rocky habitat.

In 1880, a Belgian banker named Edoardo Cahen recognized the unique beauty of the forest and bought the whole estate, which included the castle of Torre Alfina. He completely renovated the castle and built a neo-gothic mausoleum for himself in a small clearing in his beloved woods. He was buried there in the 1920s. Today, *Bosco del Sasseto* belongs to the local municipality and is only open to the public on guided tours. The castle is primarily used as a wedding venue.

Why go? The idea of a true wilderness in Italy is something that has been obsolete for a very long time. The experience of walking through a virgin, unharvested forest is quite alien to most Italians, unless they have traveled to other continents. *Bosco del Sasseto* provides a tiny window into the natural world that predates human dominance of the landscape. It is certainly unique in the region of Lazio.

 Where? *Bosco del Sasseto* is 106 kilometers north-northwest of central Rome, and 12 kilometers north of Lake Bolsena. Driving is the easiest way to get there and will take about two hours from Rome.

Cost and time? Guided tours of this special forest are only by reservation and cost €6/adult. The easy to moderate 3-kilometer nature walk takes 1.5 to 2 hours.

 Kids? The forest trails were constructed in Cahen's time and are still in good condition. They are not appropriate for strollers or wheelchairs, however, and closed-toed shoes should be worn.

 Guide? Access to *Bosco del Sasseto* is only allowed on a guided tour. Tours will set out with a minimum of ten people, so smaller numbers of visitors will be grouped together. Though the tours are typically in Italian, the guides will attempt to make concessions for English speakers.

 When? The forest is open on weekends year-round. It is also open on Fridays from April to October, and Wednesdays and Thursdays only in August. Usually there are two tours per day.

FUN FACTS

* A study conducted in 2010 found only five sites in Italian national parks that had true old-growth forest characteristics, while a further 63 showed mature forest conditions that had not yet reached real old-growth status.
* Abruzzo National Park protects Europe's oldest beech forest (50 hectares) in the *Val Cervara* outside the town of Pescasseroli. In Lazio, there is a centuries-old cork oak forest (300 hectares) in the Regional Natural Park of Monti Ausoni, outside the town of Fondi.

Enrichment: Il Barone Rampante *(1957), or* The Baron of the Trees, *is a fantastic novel by Italo Calvino that tells the story of an Italian boy who climbs a tree and never comes down. The book provides another way to imagine the forests of an earlier era. The local village of Aquapendente, which is less than 7 kilometers west of Torre Alfina, has an active street art scene, which provides a unique juxtaposition of medieval architecture with modern wall murals. Montefiascone, another adventure in this book, is 25 kilometers south of Torre Alfina.*

www.laperegina.it/bosco-sasseto-torre-alfina/

www.castellotorrealfina.com

www.percorsietruschi.it

www.prolocoacquapendente.it/acquapendente/murales/

Circeo National Park

Parco Nazionale del Circeo is one of the oldest and most diverse national parks in Italy. Founded by Benito Mussolini in 1934, the park is located along the Tyrrhenian Sea south of Rome. Specially recognized by UNESCO as a Man and the Biosphere Reserve, the park encompasses almost 9,000 hectares of land and water that protects coastal ecosystems and wildlife habitats, including sand dunes, marshes and wetlands, coastal plain forest, and the steep promontory of Mount Circeo, which stands 541 meters above the sea. The park also includes the island of Zannone, a rugged 100-hectare forested rock 28 kilometers offshore.

Why go? The unique ecosystems protected by the park are a relatively small representation of what the coastal plain must have looked like several thousand years ago before being exploited by human civilization. The park has many hiking and bicycling trails designated for exploring these natural areas. There are nature strolls through the forests, bike rides around one of the four coastal lakes, and short walks to the amazing beaches between the sand dunes. The difficulty of the hiking and biking ranges from flat and easy, to steep and hard. The trail to the promontory, for instance, is for experienced trekkers.

Where? Circeo National Park is located 87 kilometers southeast from central Rome, near the town of Sabaudia. It takes about an hour and a half to drive there, but a bus to Sabaudia from Rome-Laurentina is an option.

 Cost and time? Access to the national park is FREE, although metered parking will cost about €10/day. Given the distance from Rome and the activities you are likely seeking in the park, it will probably take a full day or weekend to enjoy.

 Kids? Absolutely, exploring nature up-close is for everyone! There is a wide diversity of wildlife to look for, including fallow deer, fox, wild boar, egrets, and flamingos.

Guide? Not needed. The park website has loads of information including lists of hiking and biking trails that include basic descriptions and maps.

 When? There are fun things to do in *Parco Nazionale del Circeo* year-round. The more difficult hikes and cycling routes might be better on nice weather days in autumn, winter, or spring, while the beach is definitely the most popular in the summertime.

FUN FACTS

* The park is named after the Greek sorceress Circe, who is known for her knowledge of herbs and potions. She also had the magical ability to turn her adversaries into animals!

* Mouflon, a wild sheep species native to the Caspian region, were introduced to Zannone in 1922 for sport hunting. They are now protected by the national park.

* Ruins of a 13th-century Cistercian monastery can be found atop Zannone.

* On the eastern shore of *Lago di Sabaudia* (a.k.a. Paola Lake) are the ruins of a villa belonging to Domitian, the Roman Emperor from 86 to 91 AD. The ruins have not yet been fully excavated and are closed to the public.

Enrichment: *If you want to learn more about Circe, she plays a role in the* Odyssey, *Homer's ancient Greek epic poem. A fun adventure that could include a visit to the island of Zannone is to hire a guided sailboat (see Adventure #XC). Sabaudia is also one of the beach adventures (#LXXXVII).*

≡ www.parcocirceo.it

Thrills

Horseback Riding

Horses have been popular in Rome from the beginning. Of course, there were the chariot races in *Circus Maximus* that attracted as many as 250,000 people. Betting on the races was a popular pastime, but the lifespans of both the horses and the chariot drivers were relatively short. Horses were also used for transportation and shipping, though very few Romans could afford them. And the Roman army used their cavalry effectively in expanding and maintaining the empire.

In modern-day Rome, horses are still visible. Carriage rides, typically popular with tourists, have recently been confined to public parks and historic villas to get them off the dangerous streets. Mounted police, most often in pairs, frequent the larger parks. And there are dozens of private riding schools, including in *Villa Borghese* and *Villa Ada*. Several stables offer the public the opportunity to ride a horse in and around Rome.

Why go? Whether you are a beginner or an experienced rider, doesn't it sound like fun to get outside in Italy and ride a horse? There are rides along *Appia Antica*, the beach at Ostia, and through the forests in the foothills. You can go for an hour or two, out for a picnic, or for a day or two. There are so many options!

 Where? Of course the riding choices vary with the location of the stable. Some are in Rome, just outside the city, and others are farther off in the countryside. It really depends on your desire and time.

 Cost and time? Again, there are many choices. There are rides that last an hour for €20, or several days for several hundred euro. Contact the individual stable for their options and rates.

Kids? This is an awesome activity for teens and tweens. Smaller kids may be too young but check with the individual stable for their age policy.

 Guide? All stables that allow public horseback riding do so only when accompanied by a reputable riding guide to ensure both the safety of the riders and the horses. Your tour guide might want to come along also to tell stories about what you're seeing.

 When? Riding centers are typically open year-round, but certainly check their availability ahead of time and make a reservation. Carriage rides in the parks are technically prohibited from noon until 5:30 pm in July and August to avoid the heat of the day. Good weather days are better for everyone! Sunset rides are beautiful.

FUN FACTS

* Emperor Caligula loved his horse, *Incitatus*, so much that it lived in an ornate marble stable, drank out of a golden bucket, and was invited to state dinners. Caligula even appointed the horse to the Senate, though probably more as a display of his power than out of affection for the pony.
* International show jumping comes to *Piazza di Siena* in *Villa Borghese* at the end of each May. It's a great chance to see powerfull horses up-close, and it's FREE.

Enrichment: *Riding a horse along the Appian Way goes right by ancient mausoleums and monuments. Horseracing has been happening at the* Ippodromo delle Capannelle *near Ciampino Airport in Rome since 1881. The track has also been home to the Rock in Roma music festival every June and July since 2009.*

≡ www.ridingancientrome.it

www.facebook.com/equestrianitaly

www.equitazione-maneggio-passeggiate-cavalli-trekking-roma.it/index
_en.asp

www.ciampacavallo.it

www.antiquitates.it/centro-ippico

www.piazzadisiena.it

www.rockinroma.com/en/

ADVENTURE #LXXXII

Ziplining

Billing itself as the longest (2,225 meters) zipline in Europe and the fastest
(up to 160 kilometers per hour) in the world, "Flying in the Sky" certainly
sets itself up to be a premier thrill ride. Also known as *Il Volo del Falco
Pellegrino*, or The Flight of the Peregrine Falcon, the zipline drops 350

meters while the rider, lying horizontal and headfirst, is flying at a maximum height over 300 meters above the olive groves. It has been open since 2014.

Why go? For the thrill of flying like a falcon!

Where? "Flying in the Sky" is based in the village of Rocca Massima, which is 43 kilometers southeast of central Rome. The easiest way to get there is to drive, but their website says that with prior arrangements they will pick you up at a nearby train station (Colleferro or Velletri) for a small fee. To avoid the wait for the shuttle, it's possible to park at the bottom and hike up to the start of the flight.

Cost and time? There are two riding options, either as a single (€39) or a tandem (€70). You can also get a video of your facial expressions during the ride for an extra €20. There is a maximum weight limit of 150 kilograms for a tandem, and a maximum weight difference between the two people in the tandem of 40 kilograms. People with disabilities are welcome. They book a ride every six minutes, and the whole drop takes about a minute. Make a

reservation before you go and be there at least an hour before your flight time for the safety talk. You may have to wait for a critical mass of people for the shuttle back to the top after your ride.

 Kids? Children must have the permission of their parents to ride.

 Guide? No guides involved, but safety is paramount, so every rider is heavily coached on what to do prior to their "flight." You are supplied with a helmet and goggles. Wear closed-toe shoes!

 When? Flying on a sunny day affords amazing views but flying through the clouds would be fun too. The zipline is closed from December to March.

FUN FACTS

* The origins of ziplining are largely unknown, but it likely started as a means to facilitate transportation through rugged terrain, like crossing steep valleys or rivers.
* Many modern ziplines have been installed in jungle forests around the world, taking advantage of the structure of tall trees and opening a window into the ecology of forest canopies.
* "Flying in the Sky" zipline is unique in that the "flyer" soars above the trees like a falcon.
* While you are flying, keep an eye out for the actual falcons that may live in the nearby mountains. You might also see griffons, a type of vulture.

Enrichment: *There are many adventures in this book in the Castelli Romani, which you have to pass through or around to get to "Flying in the Sky" ziplining. There are the hilltowns of Frascati and Arriccia, the lakes of Albano and Nemi, St. Nilo's Abbey, and the ruins of Tusculum. Farther south is the Garden of Ninfa and the three Cistercian Abbeys.*

≡ www.flyinginthesky.it/en/

Paragliding

You've probably seen those crazy people suspended from large, colorful, kite-like wings in the sky above a mountain town or along a bluff that overlooks the sea. They look a little like they're parachuting, but the fabric wing is designed to ride on the wind and the thermals created from rising warm air. It isn't jumping off something and falling slowly to the ground as much as being lifted off the ground and soaring in the wind. Paragliding has evolved from the 1960s to become a popular recreational sport, as technological advancements and standardized training have increased the safety of the activity. Many paragliding companies in Lazio offer a tandem flying experience, where a beginner, most usually the paying customer, is harnessed under the wing with a professional pilot for an exciting and panoramic flight.

Why go? If this doesn't sound like fun to you then you probably don't even need to ask this question. But if you're on the fence, soaring like a bird, riding the thermals, with nothing under your feet is an awesome feeling. And the landscape views are amazingly beautiful and exhilarating!

 Where? There are many established paraglider take-off points throughout the region but the two most actively used by commercial paragliding companies are near the village of Norma, south of Rome, and outside of Poggio Bustone, north of Rome. If you are getting there by car, the pilots/guides will generally rendezvous with you at an established meeting point and proceed to the take-off point. Some companies will pick you up at the local train station. Companies that offer paragliding include Sky Experience, Cloudhunters, Gravity, and Fly the Apennines.

 Cost and time? Paragliding companies generally classify their flights based on the planned length of time in the air, from a 15-minute introductory glide to a 90-minute cross-country excursion. Their pricing corresponds to the flight time and is similar between companies. The 15-20 minute introductory tandem flights cost around €100/person. The more extensive 90-minute cross-country flights are more like €220. Practically, with the set-up time, safety talk, and debrief, the whole adventure will take an entire afternoon. There is appropriate attire for paragliding: good shoes, eyewear, helmet, gloves, and long pants are typical.

 Kids? Some of the companies have a minimum age of 16.

 Guide? Your pilot is your guide! There is really no other way to do this adventure safely without a professional pilot/guide. Most paragliding pilots will also video the flight so that you have a souvenir you can show off to your family and friends.

When? Paragliding is highly weather dependent. The wind can be too strong, too calm, or too blustery to safely ride as a tandem. The guides will have the experience to determine when the conditions are right for your flight. But be prepared for your flight to be postponed because conditions, even at the last minute, can become unsafe. Summertime is good for paragliding, but a sunny day in the winter with snow on the ground also sounds like a fantastic experience. If you go in the wintertime, make sure to dress warm enough.

FUN FACTS

* The countries where the sport is most popular include France, Germany, Korea, and Japan.
* Paragliding differs from hang gliding in that there is no rigid structure to the wing.

Enrichment: If flying is your thing, there are also sightseeing flights that are based out of Rome Urbe Airport. A 30-minute helicopter tour starts at €240/person. You can choose flights that focus on the city, Tivoli, or Bracciano. Small plane tours start at €90/person for a 20-minute flight around Rome. Hot-air balloon excursions, based out of the village of Magliano Sabina, start at around €250/person.

www.parapendiobipostoroma.it

www.tandemparagliding-rome.com

www.flytheapennines.com

www.gravityrome.com

www.parapendiolazio.it

www.romanhomes.com/services/rome_flying_tours.htm

www.romamongolfiere.it

Skiing/Snowboarding

You may be surprised to learn that there is skiing this far south in Italy, but the Apennine Mountain range extends for over 1,200 kilometers down the center of the peninsula. The highest peaks, culminating in the Gran Sasso at 2,912 meters in elevation, are due east of Rome and receive plenty of snow in the wintertime. There are dozens of ski areas in the Apennines, mostly targeting families and beginners with only a few lifts. Though they don't really rival the destination skiing experience of the Alps and Dolomites farther north, they do provide an excellent opportunity to learn the sport and play in the snow.

Why go? If you are skier, you'll go because you can be on the snow in a little over 90 minutes from Rome; if you are not a skier, you should go because you can be playing in the snow (learning to ski) in a little over 90 minutes from Rome.

 Where? The easiest way to go skiing is with your own car. You can take what you want and come and go as you please. A close second, however, is the skibus that leaves from two locations in Rome several days per week. It leaves early in the morning and returns in the late afternoon of the same day. The bus typically goes to one of three ski areas: *Campo Felice* (88 kilometers east-northeast of Rome), *Ovindoli Monte Magnola* (88 kilometers east-northeast), or *Campo Imperatore* (105 kilometers northeast). All of the areas have their individual advantages and disadvantages, but they are all worth visiting.

 Cost and time? To be honest, there is nothing cheap about going skiing. It takes a lot of time, effort, and equipment. The skibus makes it as easy as possible, with one fee that can include the bus

ride, the lift ticket, equipment rental, and a ski lesson. The pricing gets marginally more expensive the closer to the day of the activity, but typically the bus and lift ticket is around €45/person. If you're thinking of skiing many times during a ski season, ski areas typically sell a season pass to make it more economical. Season passes at ski areas in the Apennines cost around €400/season. See the individual ski area websites for details about their prices.

 Kids? Everyone likes to play in the snow, and ski lessons can start as early as four or five years old.

 Guide? If you're new to skiing, you will need to start with lessons. All ski areas will likely have instructors and lesson options that should be prearranged before showing up at the mountain.

When? Wintertime, obviously. The best snow will be had during or just after a snowstorm, but the best views will be had on a sunny day. On the very best days, there is fresh fallen snow and clear skies. Many winter days in the central Apennines are sunny, so planning a trip during nice weather is easy.

FUN FACTS

* The ski season in the Apennines is relatively short given their latitude and relatively low elevation, and likely getting shorter due to a changing climate despite the great efforts to generate manmade snow. When the conditions are good, don't wait.
* The approach to *Campo Imperatore* from the valley bottom is via a 100-person tram that ascends 1,000 meters. Though the ski area is modest, it has fantastic views of the Gran Sasso and was the site of a daring rescue of a captive Mussolini in 1943 by Hitler's commandos.

Enrichment: *The* après ski, *or what comes after skiing, is a big part of the experience. If you are making a weekend or vacation out of your skiing adventure, this can include hot chocolate, hot tubs, and a hot meal. Many ski areas are open in the summer for mountain biking and hiking.*

www.gogobus.it

www.campofelice.it

www.ovindolimagnola.it

www.ilgransasso.it

Caving

Underground caves are formed by the weathering of rock and sediment over long periods of time largely due to moving water. Caves are most prevalent in "karst" landscapes where the geology is dominated by water-soluble rocks such as limestone, dolomite, or gypsum. These areas tend to have few surface streams since water readily percolates underground, eventually creating subsurface flows through caves and then emerging elsewhere as springs.

Caving is the exploration of cave systems, and technically, this adventure is more about visiting "tourist caves" than spelunking into "wild caves." That said, the region of Lazio has several caves that are large enough for people to explore and are open to the public on guided tours. They have names like Pastena, Collepardo, Falvaterra, Pietrasecca, and dell'Arco. They have large underground caverns with stalactites and stalagmites in interesting and beautiful shapes, made even more enchanting by installed lighting (or personal headlamps). They are cold and wet, and some of the caves have ponds, creeks, and waterfalls. Some even offer more elaborate adventures that require wetsuits and booties (Falvaterra, Pietrasecca, and dell'Arco)!

Why go? The cold and wet atmosphere of natural caves provide a unique attraction for many people. Perhaps it's the thrill of being deep underground and potentially really in the dark, or maybe it is the primordial link to some of our earliest shelters. Indeed, human artifacts have been found in *Grotta di Collepardo* that date to 3,500 years ago, and *Grotta dell'Arco* has rock paintings from 3,000 to 4,000 BC. Of course, there is a grandeur to the natural beauty of the eroded caverns and the growing rock formations, particularly in the shadowy light.

Tiziana Ceccarelli

Where? All of these caves are in rural mountainous areas and will require a car to reach efficiently. *Grotta di Pastena*, for example, is the farthest one of these caves from central Rome at 95 kilometers southeast.

 Cost and time? The cost of a guided cave tour generally varies with how long the tour takes and how deep into the cave the tour goes. Basic tours cost in the range of €7-9 and take about an hour. The tours that require people to get wet cost €20-35 and take two or three hours. Rental of the wetsuits may be extra. Check the individual websites for details.

 Kids? The basic tours are generally open to people of all ages, provided they aren't afraid of the dark or confined spaces. Some of the caves have constructed walkways, while others do not. The more elaborate trips may have age restrictions (check websites). Caves are also habitat for unusual species of insects and many species of bats, so there's that.

 Guide? Public access to all of these caves is only on a guided tour with professional guides. No one wants to get lost in there!

 When? Opening times vary between caves, and some are only open on weekends. They tend to be more active in the summer months, as the cool caves provide an excellent break from the hot summer temperatures. There is some seasonality to the access, particularly the caves that have flowing water, and they may be closed during the rainy season when the water is running high. Check the websites for details.

FUN FACTS

＊ Caving is also known as potholing.

＊ Amazing caves can be found all over the world. The deepest known cave, at 2,197 meters, is the Kubera Cave in the country of Georgia. Mammoth Cave, in the United States, is the longest known cave at almost 590 kilometers, but not all of it has been explored yet. The largest cave chamber by surface area, at almost 155,000 square meters, is the Mulu Cave in Malaysia. That is big enough to hold 40 Boeing 747 airplanes!

Enrichment: *Surface-level sinkholes occur when an underground cave collapses.* Il Pozzo d'Antullo *is a natural sinkhole not far from* Grotta di Collepardo. *It is 140 meters wide and 60 meters deep. Stalactites grow from the overhanging wall and vegetation grows in the bottom. Legend has it that shepherds lowered their sheep into the pit to graze for months at a time. The sinkhole is now a tourist attraction.*

www.grottepastenacollepardo.it

www.comune.carsoli.aq.it/archivio17_turismo-luoghi-da-visitare_o_1.html

www.grottedifalvaterra.it

www.grottedellarco.com

PART FOUR

Aquatic Adventures

The Sea Beaches

Cancello 2: Free Beach

Ostia is primarily known as Rome's beach town, and the sand extends for 40 kilometers southeast all the way to Anzio. In the summertime, that long stretch attracts thousands of sun worshippers. The sun is hot, the water is warm, and beach clubs have nicely laid out sun chairs (*lettini*) and umbrellas (*ombrelloni*) that are available to rent.

Cancello 2, or Gate 2, is just one of the beaches along that stretch that provides a classic Mediterranean beach experience as a day trip from Rome. Upon arrival, you are greeted at the beach club/restaurant on the edge of the sand where you are assigned an umbrella and sun chairs, and where you will return periodically for food, cold drinks, and gelato. The beach attendant will show you the way. Then you will spend the rest of the day swimming, reading, sleeping, rolling over, and moving your chair back into the shade of the umbrella. Relax already!

Why go? Because it's summertime on the Mediterranean Sea! There is nothing particularly special about *Cancello* 2, there is also a *Cancello* 1, *Cancello* 3, 4, 5, 6, 7, and 8. A little farther up the beach is *Varco* (or passage) 1, 2, 3, 4, and 5. *Cancello* 7 is LGBTQ friendly and Capocotta beach, at *Varco* 3, is for "naturists." All of these places will provide similar services. It is possible, of course, to go to the beach and not partake in these services; there is FREE open beach between the clubs. But it's so much easier going to the beach when the chair and umbrella are waiting for you.

Where? *Cancello* 2 is 25 kilometers south-southwest of central Rome. The easiest way to get is there is by car (*Via Litoranea 1350*) and it takes about an hour. Though there is a lot of parking, on summer weekends it can be scarce, as both off-road spots beyond the gate and those along the road fill up by midday. Get there early. Of course there's no need to be wedded to *Cancello* 2 — keep going until you find a parking spot.

Public transit can get you there too, as there is a public bus that runs along the seafront road. The local train from Rome to the coast at Ostia ends at Station Cristoforo Colombo (€1.50), which is also a beach destination. And then take the local bus (€1.50) southeast along the sea toward Torvajanica. *Cancello* 2 has a designated stop, as do the other *cancellos*.

 Cost and time? Two sunbeds and an umbrella can be rented for €18 per day, which is typical. The food and drink at the restaurant are also modestly priced. Stay as long as you want.

 Kids? Yes, it's the beach! Generally, in the summer there are little, if any, waves and the depth of water increases very gradually. If you forget the beach toys there are vendors strolling the beach with all the options. Some beach clubs have lifeguards.

 Guide? Nope.

 When? The beach season on the Mediterranean is quite long, stretching from May to September. The hotter it gets the more crowded the beach gets. And, of course, the weekends are the most crowded and the demand for chairs and umbrellas is high. You should also consider that most of Rome leaves the city for the beach in August. Though the restaurant at the free beach is open year-round, it might be good to call to check if you plan to go in the off-season.

FUN FACTS

＊ Beach vendors stroll the beach selling everything from sunglasses to kites to jewelry.

✳ Flip-flops will allow you to walk from your umbrella to the water without burning the bottoms of your feet.

✳ Italians can discreetly change their beach clothes under their towels and can arrive and depart the beach looking quite elegant.

Enrichment: *Being a peninsula, Italy is nearly surrounded by beaches. Each has its own characteristics and it would take more than a lifetime to see them all. Sardinia, Sicily, Calabria, Tuscany, Puglia . . . there are famous beaches everywhere. And most Italians love to go to the beach, often having a second family house near one of them to facilitate the summer getaway.*

≡ www.castelporziano.com

Sabaudia

Sabaudia is a coastal town southeast of Rome built from scratch after Mussolini drained large areas of marsh to create farmland. *Lungomare di*

Sabaudia is 23 kilometers of Mediterranean Sea beaches in Circeo National Park, which incorporates the town of Sabaudia and stretches from Circeo Mountain in the southeast to just past *Lago di Fogliano* in the northwest. The park is also a UNESCO "Man and the Biosphere Reserve" because of its unique coastal dunes, wetlands, and forest. The beaches span the gamut from protected undeveloped swaths where beachgoers must be totally self-sufficient, to the typical Italian beach club with sun chair and umbrella rentals. The density of beach clubs decreases the farther northwest you go.

Why go? The biggest reason to make the journey to Sabaudia is to walk on a designated trail from the coastal road through the protected dunes and down to an undeveloped beach and spend the day away from the typical Italian beach crowds. It's the anti-beach club experience, though there will likely still be other people around. Of course, you'll have to bring your own shade and refreshments, but it's much more of a "meeting nature" experience.

 Where? Though it's possible to get to Sabaudia by a combination of train and bus, it is much easier to get there with a car. The town of Sabaudia is 80 kilometers southeast of Rome and it takes at

least an hour and a half to get there. Access to the less-developed beaches at the northwestern end of the *Lungomare di Sabaudia* is limited by drainage canals and may require some extra navigation.

 Cost and time? There is a parking fee (€5) along most of the *Lungomare di Sabaudia* but the beach itself is FREE, unless you choose the beach club option.

 Kids? Kids love the beach!

 Guide? No

 When? Summertime, or really anytime that the weather is nice. On stormy days the beach can be spectacular and lonely.

FUN FACTS

* Some beaches on the northwestern end of the *Lungomare di Sabaudia* are not accessible directly via the coastal road and require a longer hike along a trail. At the south end of the beaches is a stretch of expensive houses on the bluff overlooking the sea.
* The planned town of Sabaudia is known for its unique Fascist-era architecture.
* The UNESCO Man and the Biosphere Program started in 1971 and there are now more than 700 reserves in over 125 countries.

Enrichment: A surfing community has evolved at the southern end of the beach to take advantage of the waves, especially in the storm season. It's possible to hike to the top of the Circeo Promontory at the southern end of the park, though it's not easy. You will need the right shoes and it's not for those who are afraid of heights. There is also a less daunting nature trail through the botanical gardens.

☰ www.parcocirceo.it/index.php

Fregene

Fregene is coastal town just to the north of Fiumicino Airport. It has nearly 5 kilometers of beautiful sea beaches and over 20 beach clubs. Originally, it was an ancient Etruscan seaport at the mouth of the Arrone River, and more recently it was a tiny fishing village. When the surrounding marshy area was drained in the 1920s, the town became known for its beaches and its close proximity to the city of Rome. Today, Romans come to Fregene beaches for the day, and many people have second homes in the community to get away from the city in the summer.

Why go? Fregene offers the classic Italian summer beach experience of lying around on a rented reclining sun chair in the shade of a rented umbrella and periodically cooling off in the calm warm sea. Many of the beach clubs also have pools. There are FREE portions of the beach for those not wanting to rent equipment. The beach clubs are also excellent places for a sunset *aperitivo* and there are some nice seafood restaurants if you stay for dinner (try the *spaghetti con le telline*), particularly in the fishermen's village at the north end of the beach. There are typically fewer people on the beaches of Fregene than the beaches of Ostia.

 Where? The beach at Fregene is about 25 kilometers west of the center of Rome. It takes roughly 45 minutes to drive there. A train from Rome-Termini goes to Maccarese-Fregene in about 35 minutes, where a local bus goes the last 5 kilometers to the beach.

 Cost and time? Renting two chairs and an umbrella for the day shouldn't cost more than €20. How long you stay depends on you.

 Kids? Yes! If you forget the sand toys there will likely be a vendor not too far away. The beach clubs typically have lifeguards on duty.

 Guide? No

When? Summertime, although walks on the deserted beach in the wintertime are fun too. You will likely get a spot closer to the water (and a parking place) if you go earlier in the day. Locals and regulars with annual beach club memberships usually already have some of the best spots reserved. There will be fewer people during the week than on weekends.

FUN FACTS

* In addition to the sun chair and umbrella rentals, Italian beach clubs usually have changing rooms, toilets, showers, and restaurants. Some have other kinds of recreation too, like beach volleyball, paddleboats, and windsurfing.

* Many Italians spend their entire summer vacation at the beach. Indeed, by the *Ferragosto* holiday on August 15th, much of Rome is emptied of locals and a vacant sun chair at the beach is hard to find.

* Federico Fellini lived here! The last scene of *La Dolce Vita* (1960) was filmed on the beach.

Enrichment: *At the south end of Fregene beach is a 280-hectare nature reserve owned and managed by the World Wildlife Fund called the Macchiagrande Oasis. With over 7 kilometers of flat public hiking trails through several types of ecosystems, including sand dunes, wetlands, and coastal pine forest, it's possible to see herons, kestrels, beech martins, and tortoises. Fregene is also close to Portus and on the way to the Etruscan Necropolis at Cerveteri, which are both adventures in this book.*

☰ www.visitfiumicino.com/tour_categories/fregene/?lang=en

ADVENTURE #LXXXIX

Santa Severa

Santa Severa is a beach town northwest of Rome. Its origins date back to the Etruscans, who established a port called *Pyrgi* at the site as early as the 5th century BC. The current name comes from a Christian who was martyred on the beach at the end of the 3rd century AD. Pope Leo IV built a fortified tower and castle at the suspected martyrdom site in the 9th century, and it was periodically renovated through the 17th century.

Today, Santa Severa is a classic Italian beach town. In the summer there are many beach clubs renting reclining chairs and umbrellas, and restaurants with beautiful views of the sea. What sets it apart from other beach towns, however, is the castle at the south end of the beach. The castle itself is now the Civic Museum of Sea and Ancient Navigation. The medieval village adjacent to the castle has craftsmen shops, the Antiquarium Museum with Etruscan artifacts, a visitor center for the local nature reserve, a modern hostel, and a beer pub.

Why go? There aren't many places in the world where you can go to the beach at the base of a medieval castle. It is visually stunning! There are also all of the activities in the old village itself.

Where? Santa Severa is 46 kilometers northwest of central Rome and 15 kilometers southeast of the port of Civitavecchia. Of course, the easiest way to get there from Rome is by car, but a train goes to Santa Severa almost every hour, takes about 40 minutes, and costs about €3/person each way. It's a little over a kilometer walk from the train station to the castle and the beach, or you could catch a taxi.

 Cost and time? The beach is FREE if you bring all your own stuff. Renting a couple of chairs and an umbrella from a beach club typically costs less than €20 for the day. The museum in the castle costs €8/adult. It's easy to spend the whole day here.

Kids? Of course! Kids at the beach: perfect. Combine with a castle and some history: even more perfect!

 Guide? There are guided tours of the castle and village for €6/person. There are also audio guides in English to rent for €5.

 When? Summertime, though the castle and village are open year-round (except Mondays). The beach can get quite crowded on summer weekends. In the winter, you can walk down the beach almost by yourself, but you won't get much of a tan.

~~~~~~~~~~~~~~~~~~~~~~~~~~~~~~~~

FUN FACTS

* Santa Severa regularly hosts a surfing festival in July.
* The museum in the castle focuses on the role that seafaring played in the ancient Etruscan and Roman societies.
* Three golden Etruscan tablets were found in 1964 when excavating two beachfront temples at the *Pyrgi* archeological site, which is just south of the castle. They greatly enhanced current understanding of the Etruscan language and are currently in the National Etruscan Museum at *Villa Giulia* in Rome.

~~~~~~~~~~~~~~~~~~~~~~~~~~~~~~~~

Enrichment: *If you are interested in the ancient Etruscans, there are many archeological sites along the northern Lazio coast, including the necropoli at Cerveteri and Tarquinia, and the ruins of the city of Vulci, all of which are adventures in this book.*

≡ www.castellodisantasevera.it/en/

Sailing

The idea of chartering a sailboat in Italy sounds like a posh vacation only for professional athletes and CEOs, but it doesn't have to be that way. There are many relatively economical opportunities to enjoy the Tyrrhenian Sea by boat. This can mean a sunset *aperitivo* sail, a weekend cruise down the Lazio coast, or a week of exploration in the Pontine Islands. Boat captains and chartering companies have set itineraries to choose from or they can customize voyages to specific limitations in time and budget.

The Pontine Islands are lesser known to foreigners than Sicily and Capri, but they are certainly no less beautiful. They are six rocky islands about 25 kilometers offshore of Lazio. Ponza is the largest, and one of only two of the Pontines that are inhabited year-round, with about 3,500 residents. The other populated island is Ventotene, which has just over 700 people and no cars. Both have excellent restaurants and hotels. Palmarola Island has great natural beauty and a few seasonal restaurants, and was the favorite Mediterranean island of Jacques Cousteau. The other three islands are much smaller and have ruins of human habitation but

Miceli Vela

are currently only visited by people on day tours. Santo Stefano has the remains of an old prison, Zannone is part of the Circeo National Park, and Gavi, a steep wildlife refuge, is only 16 hectares in size.

Why go? There are three big reasons why you should try sailing in Lazio. The first is that there are many amazing, secluded beaches and sea grottos that are only accessible by boat. The beaches have the clear blue water the Mediterranean is famous for and a long, varied history that extends from pirates to romance. The second reason is that cruising down the Lazio coast will give you the unique perspective that roman sailors had for millennia while supplying ancient Rome with goods from around the empire. And the third reason for sailing in Lazio is that it truly is a dream vacation: warm sun, beautiful sea, clear blue water, and maybe an evening visit from a floating bartender who plies the more popular mooring bays.

 Where? Sailboat charters are possible from many of the Lazio sea-ports: Civitavecchia, Ostia, Anzio, Nettuno, Terracina, Gaeta, and Formia. Many of these towns can be reached by local train lines.

 Cost and time? The cost of sailing varies by the length of the cruise. A sunset sail lasting a couple of hours starts at about €35/person. Weeklong trips start at about €2,000 for a boat that has three cabins, each with a double berth. This price is only for the basics and doesn't include other necessities like food and sheets, so ask some friends to join you and budget accordingly.

 Kids? A boat is a bit stressful for parents of little kids, but certainly older kids who are confident swimmers will love this adventure. Even if there are life jackets for everyone, you are still the lifeguard on duty.

 Guide? The boat captain is your guide! And you will undoubtedly learn something about the science of sailing. You can also arrange local guides and tours at ports-of-call to help flesh out the experience.

When? Summer is the best time to go, when you can jump into the beautiful blue water the moment you are hot. In the winter, the air and water temperatures are cooler and there is an increased probability of inclement weather, but there will be much less boat traffic. The shoulder seasons of May to mid-June and mid-September to October may provide the best of both and be cheaper than the high summer season.

FUN FACTS

* It is possible to see dolphins while sailing along the Lazio coast, particularly in the winter months.
* Some of the beaches in the Pontines are closed to people due to the danger posed by rocks falling from nearby crumbling cliffs.
* The population of Ponza peaked in the 1930s at about 7,000 people. This was primarily due to Mussolini exiling his political opponents to the prison there.
* In addition to Ponza and Santo Stefano, Ventotene was also once used as a penitentiary. Indeed, Emperor Augustus imprisoned his own daughter on Ventotene, at his summer residence that became known as *Villa Giulia.*

Enrichment: Some sailing charters specialize in tours of ancient archeological sites. Powerboat charters are also available from these same port towns to the same destinations, but they are a less traditional means of sea conveyance.

www.micelivela.it/charter

www.archeosail.it

www.prometeosailing.com/index.php

www.barcarmonia.wordpress.com

www.sailinginitalycharter.it

The Lakes

Lago di Bolsena

Lago di Bolsena is the largest lake in Lazio and the biggest volcanic lake in Europe. Thirteen kilometers long, oval in shape, and covering 11,350 hectares, the lake is known for its cool, clear water with a maximum depth of 150 meters. The shore around the lake is generally low and sandy, which makes it inviting to summer beachgoers. There are three main towns on the shores of the lake (Bolsena, Marta, and Capodimonte), and several others in the surrounding hills (namely Montefiascone, Valentano, and Gradoli). There are also two small private islands in the lake (Bisentina and Martana). The Marta River flows out of the south end of the lake all the way to the sea at Tarquinia. The lands surrounding the lake are primarily agricultural, producing olives, grapes, grains, and hazelnuts.

People have been living around Lake Bolsena since the Neolithic Age (3,500 to 10,000 BC). Of course, it was also important to the Etruscans and Romans, with the latter building *Via Cassia* along the eastern side of lake, connecting it directly to Rome. The wetlands along the shore of the lake provided issues for the inhabitants, however, since they were also ripe with malarial mosquitoes. The Farnese family ruled the Duchy of Castro in the 16th century, which included much of the shore around the lake. Though it only lasted for a century, the Duchy resulted in fortresses and palaces being built in many of the area's villages. Today, Lake Bolsena is mainly known as a summer tourist destination.

Why go? *Lago di Bolsena* has beautiful, narrow dark sand beaches and shallow clear water that is perfect for cooling off in the summertime. There are many beach clubs to choose from around the lake, particularly near the towns. But there are also many FREE beaches, where beach goers are self-supported. The west coast is typically more solitary. Unlike most other lakes in Lazio, motorboats are allowed on Lake Bolsena with size restrictions. That means that there is the possibility of waterskiing, fishing, and touring around the islands. There are also schools for sailing and windsurfing. Many cafés and restaurants are sprinkled around the lake, often specializing in locally caught fish, as well as hotels, *agriturismi*, and campgrounds.

 Where? Lake Bolsena is 84 kilometers northwest of central Rome. It takes about an hour and 45 minutes to drive there. Trains from Rome-Termini can get you to Montefiascone in 90 minutes, but it is still 6 kilometers to the lake (by taxi or local bus).

 Cost and time? Because of the distance from Rome, *Lago di Bolsena* makes for a great summer weekend destination. The cost will depend on the length of the stay. Hiring a couple of sun chairs and an umbrella at a beach club will cost about €20/day.

Kids? Of course, especially during summertime at the beach!

 Guide? The town of Bolsena has several cultural attractions that could benefit from having a guide tell their stories.

 When? Summertime! The water is typically calmest in the morning when there isn't much wind. But later in the day the winds tend to pick up, making swimming and boating a little less comfortable. People engaged in the sailing sports, however, will love the afternoons.

FUN FACTS

* Amalasuntha, Queen of the Goths, was murdered by her cousin on Martana Island in 535 AD. This precipitated the last of the Gothic wars, from 535 to 553, when the Byzantine Empire invaded the Italian peninsula.

* The island of Bisentina has a dungeon (*Malta dei Papi*) for heretics that dates to the early 14th century. It is mentioned by Dante in the third part (Paradiso, Canto IX) of his epic poem, *The Divine Comedy.*

* The lake continues to provide important habitat for migratory birds, though native fauna is threatened by competition with introduced species, many from North America. The water quality of the lake is also threatened by effluent from the surrounding villages and agricultural fertilizer used in hazelnut plantations.

Enrichment: *The town of Bolsena has several cultural attractions including the Basilica of Santa Cristina, a catacomb, and a museum in the castle. This book contains many varied adventures near Lake Bolsena, including Montefiascone, Civita di Bagnoregio,* Lago di Mezzano, *Orvieto, and Bosco del Sasseto.*

www.lagodibolsena.org

www.visitbolsena.it

Lago di Mezzano

Lago di Mezzano is the shy little brother of *Lago di Bolsena*. Located less than 8 kilometers west of the big lake, Mezzano Lake also has volcanic origins but is only 48 hectares in size. Surrounded by oak forest and agricultural lands, there is limited public access. The closest town is Latera, which is 5 kilometers away.

Why go? The seclusion of this beautiful little lake is exactly what makes it so attractive. In July and August, a local outdoor education group (*Percorsi Etruschi*) runs inner tubing trips to paddle around the lake and educate the public about aquatic ecology while playing in the water. There is an *agriturismo* on the north side of the lake that has exclusive access to that portion of the waterfront. If small and secluded is what you're after in a freshwater beach, this is the place!

Where? *Lago di Mezzano* is 99 kilometers northwest of Rome. The only way to get there really is by car, and it will take about two hours from *Piazza Venezia*. The final roads are a little bumpy.

Cost and time? The lake is far enough from Rome to make it a long and uncomfortable day trip, so an adventure here will likely be at least a weekend. Check with *Percorsi Etruschi* about the cost of the tubing. Room rates at the *agriturismo* start at €40/person/night or €325/week.

Kids? The tubing tour is specifically geared toward older kids looking to cool off in the summer.

Guide? Yes, because access to the lake is limited without one (*Percorsi Etruschi*).

Percorsi Etruschi

 When? Summer! The regular aquatrekking tours (tubing) occur on Tuesdays and Saturdays but can be prearranged for any other day of the week.

FUN FACTS

✳ Divers in Mezzano Lake found the ruins of a small village on stilts that dates back to the copper age (i.e., 5,000 years ago).

✳ There used to be a Castle of Mezzano on the shores of the lake, but it was destroyed in the 14th century AD.

Enrichment: The medieval town of Latera has a 15th-century fortress built by the Farnese family. The town, which has had a declining population since the 1930s, is also known for its four fountains that mark the district neighborhoods.

www.percorsietruschi.it/itinerari/emozioni-in-natura/tubing-sul-lago -di-mezzano

www.agriturismomezzano.com/en

www.fraviaco.com/en

Lago di Vico

Lake Vico (*Lago di Vico*) is a 1,290-hectare crater lake in northern Lazio. At 500 meters in elevation, it often has cooler temperatures than in Rome. Land in the crater surrounding the lake has been excellent for hazelnut cultivation, though the Lake Vico Nature Reserve limits further commercial development. There is a small vacation community (*Punta del Lago*) on the south shore of the lake, and two on the crater rim (*Poggio Cavaliere* and *San Rocco Punta del Lago*).

Why go? Generally, there is limited public access to the water itself. But there is a hotel and an *agriturismo* on the north side of the lake that rent beach chairs and umbrellas. Adjacent to the hotel is a small public access area for self-supported beach goers. There are also several restaurants with good views at various points on the road around the lake, as well as trekking in the nature reserve.

 Where? *Lago di Vico* is 53 kilometers northeast of Rome and 17 kilometers north of *Lago di Bracciano*. A car is really the only way to get there efficiently.

 Cost and time? Going to Lake Vico from Rome is probably a full-day proposition, though there are other adventures in this book that are not too far away and could be added along the way. How much it costs depends on you: paying for beach access, eating in a restaurant, staying in the hotel, etc. The public beach is FREE.

 Kids? Absolutely.

 Guide? Nope.

 When? Summertime, when it's too hot in Rome!

* The lake was likely larger before the Etruscans drained it with an emissary (tunnel) for irrigation outside of the crater and to increase the arable farmland within the crater.
* Today's hazelnut orchards, which help feed the world's appetite for Nutella, also use water from the lake for irrigation.

Enrichment:

Hiking the nearby small peaks of *Monte Fogliano* and *Monte Venere* is possible. The latter is home to a *faggeta depressa*, or an unusually low-elevation beech forest. There are also bird blinds at various points around the lake for bird watchers. For a diverse lesson in the history of the area around *Lago di Vico*, the other adventures in this book include Marturanum, the ruins of an ancient Etruscan city and necropolis, and *Palazzo Farnese* at Caprarola, a beautiful Renaissance palace. The ancient Etruscan and Roman town of Sutri, known for its amphiteater, is less than 10 kilometers south of the lake.

≡ www.labellavenere.it
≡ www.agriturismolagentile.com

Susannah McGuire

Lago di Bracciano

Lake Bracciano is the second-largest freshwater lake in the region of Lazio at 5,676 hectares (32 kilometers in circumference). It has volcanic origins and currently serves as a source of drinking water for the City of Rome, necessitating the prohibition of most motorboats. There are three towns adjacent to the lake, including Bracciano, Anguillara Sabazia, and Trevignano Romano. Medieval Anguillara Sabazia has a promenade along the water and a town beach. Bracciano is on the crater rim and is known for its 15th-century castle. It's a short walk downhill from the village to the waterfront, which is lined with restaurants and beach clubs. Regional parks also provide public access to the lake for swimming.

Why go? Summertime in Rome is hot and Lake Bracciano is a great way to escape the city for some relief. Swimming and sunbathing are the primary summer activities. You can rent an umbrella and reclining chairs at one of the many beach clubs or bring your own to the parks. The lake is also known for sailing and there are sailboats and windsurfers for hire at various locations, as well as lessons. *Castello di Bracciano* is worth a visit, and

there are many restaurants in all three towns that have great views of the lake (or castle).

Where? Lake Bracciano is roughly 29 kilometers northwest of Centro. A car will provide the best access to the lake, but a local train also links the towns of Bracciano and Anguillara Sabazia to Rome-Termini. There are as many as 32 trains per day and they only take about 90 minutes. From Bracciano train station to the beach is about a kilometer, which you could walk, or there are plenty of taxis at the station if you prefer. You'll go right by the castle either way. The local bus goes from the train station in Anguillara Sabazia directly to the beach. Getting to Trevignano Romano is more of a challenge since it's not on the train line.

Cost and time? Going to this beach can take as much or as little time as you choose: a full-day excursion, a half-day of relaxation, or a quick sunset swim. The train is relatively cheap at only €4/person and renting an umbrella and a couple of chairs at a beach club should be about €20. Castle entry is €8.50/adult. Staying for dinner at one of the nearby restaurants increases the investment, but it's well worth it.

Kids? This is where many a Roman family spends their entire summer vacation, so it is very kid-friendly. From the water-based playground of inflatables to the summer sailing camps, this place is made for kids. The water is fresh and warm, the beach is sandy and gradual, and the gelato is never too far away.

Guide? Once you figure out Italian beach etiquette (perhaps an idea for another book), you're good to go. The second visit is even easier. The castle has guided tours to help with the centuries of stories.

When? Summer!

FUN FACTS

✳ Pasta made with fresh fish caught from the lake is a local delicacy.

✳ Everyone knows about the celebrity weddings at the castle (e.g., Tom Cruise), but did you know that the American TV show *Everybody Loves Raymond* shot some episodes in Anguillara Sabazia?

~~~~~~~~~~~~~~~~

Enrichment: *There is an* agriturismo *on the east side of the lake that offers water access in the summertime and fresh products from their farm. A summer ferry links the three villages around the lake and provides a nice sightseeing excursion for €10/person round-trip. Many scuba diving schools teach their lessons in Lake Bracciano off of the beach at Trevignano Romano. There are a couple of submerged miniature model ships for divers to "discover." There are also the ruins of* La Marmotta *village at the bottom of the lake near Anguillara Sabazia, which date from 7500 BC.*

www.odescalchi.it

www.aziendaagricolapolline.it

www.consorziolagodibracciano.it

ADVENTURE #XCV

Lago di Martignano

Lake Martignano is Lake Bracciano's little sibling, being only 244 hectares in size (6 kilometers around) and 2 kilometers east. It is also a crater lake but has little development nearby. There is public beach access along the south side of Martignano, and private beach club access on the north side. Generally, it has a more laid-back vibe than Bracciano.

Why go? Though it's still possible to rent canoes and paddleboats during the summer, the commercial ventures near Lake Martignano are on a much smaller scale than Lake Bracciano. The water increases in depth very gradually (good for little kids), and there is a large lawn to spread out to enjoy the sun.

Where? Lake Martignano is 27 kilometers north-northwest of central Rome and you will need a car to get there. Not only that, since it is located in a regional park, there is no direct vehicle access to the shore that is open to the public. Visitors must park in one of the designated parking lots (some cost €5/car) and take a private shuttle (€2/person) or walk to the lake. This extra hurdle helps keep the summertime crowds down. One of the parking lots is on the outskirts of the village of Anguillara Sabazia.

Cost and time? Since getting to the lake takes some effort, you will probably want to spend the day. The costs once you're there, however, are quite modest. If you're able to park close and walk, it's possible to do it for FREE.

Kids? Hiking down the hill from the parking lot to the lake and back are the obvious limitations for kids, but using the shuttle is easy. Once you're at the lake, it is a great place for all ages.

Guide? A guide is not needed, though figuring out how to get there will be a challenge the first time.

When? Summer! In the off-season and when the weather is still decent, it's good to arrive a little more self-sufficient, as there may or may not be chairs, umbrellas, or food available.

FUN FACTS

* In the time of Emperor Augustus (around 2 BC), water from Lake Martignano was brought to Rome via the *Aqua Alsietina* aqueduct to be used in staged naval battles for public entertainment in a custom-built stadium in Trastevere, called a *naumachia*. How crazy is that?
* A scientific study of pollen from core samples taken from the bottom of Lake Martignano indicates that arable crops were present in the basin from at least 3500 BC.

Enrichment: *The couple of* agriturismi *on the north side of the lake also provide access to the water. This is an excellent alternative to the public beach, though they will cost some money. They also have horseback riding and a designated dog beach!*

www.parcobracciano.it
www.agriturismoilcastoro.it
www.casaledimartignano.it

Lago del Turano

Lago del Turano is a reservoir in the hills northeast of Rome. The small, picturesque medieval village of *Castel di Tora* overlooks the lake on the north side, and the newer town of *Colle di Tora* is across a one-lane bridge on the south side. A dam built in 1938 created the reservoir, which is roughly 10 kilometers long and up to 60 meters deep. Because of the steep valley walls and varying water depth, access to the water is somewhat limited, but that has not deterred a growing community based on summer recreation — namely swimming, sunbathing, fishing, and various kinds of non-motorized watercraft.

Why go? When it's hot in Rome, head to *Lago del Turano*! The beauty is amazing. Plus, you don't often find a good swimming hole underneath a castle in a hilltop Italian village. There are several beach club type places that rent chairs and umbrellas, and boathouses that rent pedal boats and kayaks. You can also find public water access where the rocky beach is not as steep.

 Where? Lake Turano is 52 kilometers northeast of Rome and it takes about 90 minutes to get there by car.

 Cost and time? This is probably a day trip or overnight from Rome, once you've walked through *Castel di Tora,* relaxed in the sun (about €20 to rent an umbrella and a couple of chairs), and pedaled a boat (about €10/hour) across the lake to swim on the other side. There are several restaurants that overlook the water from the two villages, including two fun places in the old hilltop part of *Castel di Tora.*

 Kids? The kids will love it here with the swimming and the boats. The water gets deep quite quickly, so be careful!

 Guide? No guide is needed for the lake unless you want to walk up to the *Borgo Antuni*, a castle on a hilltop adjacent to *Castel di Tora* that was accidentally bombed during WWII. Guided walks up to the restored castle are €6/person.

 When? Summer.

FUN FACTS

* The Turano Dam is 80 meters high and 256 meters across.
* Water from the Turano reservoir flows north through a 9-kilometer tunnel to the Salto reservoir. From the Salto, the water flows north through an additional 11 kilometers of tunnels until gravity helps it generate electricity at a power plant outside the village of Cittaducale. The water ultimately ends up in the Velino River upstream of the town of Rieti.

Enrichment: There is good hiking in the hills above the Lago del Turano, *including to a waterfall. For more committed trekkers, the* Cammino di Benedetto *passes right through* Castel di Tora. *Caving at* Grotte di Pietrasecca *is also not far from the lake.*

www.navegnacervia.it

www.camminandocon.org

www.camminodibenedetto.it

Lago Albano

Lago Albano is perhaps the most well-known lake in Lazio because of its proximity to Castel Gandolfo, the town that hosts the summer residence of the pope. The volcanic lake, which is located south of Rome in the *Castelli Romani*, also played host to the rowing and canoeing events at the 1960 Summer Olympics. Of course, the ancient Romans also used Lake Albano, having built a 1,450-meter irrigation tunnel (emissary) in 395 BC that went through the crater rim to reach the fields on the other side. They came to the lake to escape the summer heat of the city, much the same way modern Romans do today. Artifacts have been found at the lake, including stilt houses, which show human use of the lake as far back as the 20th century BC.

Lago Albano is about 600 hectares in size and 170 meters deep. The towns of Castel Gandolfo and Albano Laziale are above the lake on the crater rim to the west and southwest, respectively. Castel Gandolfo, in particular, has fantastic views of the lake. The northern shore of the lake has been developed into beach clubs, while the south shore is forested and is accessed via a 6-kilometer semi-loop trail for walking and biking. The trail is replaced at the top of the lake by 4 kilometers of road, which is not particularly pedestrian friendly.

Why go? People have been recreating at Lake Albano for millennia, attracted by the cool water and dark sand beaches. Today, in addition to the sunbathing and swimming afforded by the beach clubs, there are all manner of boats available to rent, as long as they don't have a motor: pedal boats, kayaks, sailboats, windsurfers, canoes, and rowing shells. The hike/bike around the southern part of the lake affords great views, and there are restaurants and cafés associated with some of the beach clubs at the north end. There are also group kayak tours around the lake that are followed by a wine *aperitivo*!

 Where? *Lago Albano* is 21 kilometers southeast of central Rome. It will take about 45 minutes to drive there from *Piazza Venezia*. A train also goes from Rome-Termini to Albano Laziale, which also stops at Castel Gandolfo. It's possible to walk downhill or take a taxi from the station to the lake.

 Cost and time? Spending the whole day at Lake Albano with all the activities available is easy, and that's not even counting Castel Gandolfo. The beach clubs will rent a couple of sun chairs and an umbrella for less than €20 for the day. Kayak rentals start at €10/ hour, and a kayak-*aperitivo* tour of the lake starts at €60/person.

Kids? Yes, absolutely. From the swimming at the beach to walking or bicycling on the trail, all kids will enjoy *Lago Albano*.

 Guide? Recreationally, a guide is not needed to enjoy the lake. For the kayak tour, however, the guide is an integral part of the experience. Make sure to make a reservation ahead of time. A guide is also invaluable for a tour of the neighboring villages of the *Castelli Romani*.

 When? The beach is best enjoyed during the warmer part of the year (April to October), but the trail along the south side of the lake is good year-round. The wind can pick up in the afternoon making kayaking and canoeing a little more challenging.

FUN FACTS

* Precipitation is the sole input of water into Lake Albano and its surface level has been dropping for several decades. This likely has an impact on the water quality of the lake, as periodic swimming closures have also occurred.
* There are both native and introduced fish species in the lake.

Enrichment: *The first pope to stay at the Papal Palace of Castel Gandolfo was Urban VIII in 1628. Papal interest in the palace has ebbed and flowed over time, as some popes invested in its improvement and others did not. The French severely damaged the palace in 1778. However, 55 hectares of gardens have been added recently. The current pope (Francis) does not use the palace, which makes it possible for public tours of the Papal apartments and the gardens. The Two Popes (2019) is a movie that takes an interesting look at the relationship between Pope Benedict XVI and Pope Francis.*

www.comune.castelgandolfo.rm.it
www.ckacademy.it/en/

Lago di Nemi

Lago di Nemi is one of the smallest (167 hectares) volcanic lakes in Lazio and just over the ridge from Lake Albano in the *Castelli Romani* (the hills southeast of Rome). There are two towns on the crater's rim, Nemi and Genzano di Roma. The lake has a long history: there's a 5th century BC temple nearby built to honor the goddess Diana of the Wood, and the lake was home to Caligula's party ships in the 1st century AD.

Today, a paved road goes most of the way around the lake, but the unpaved portion is connected with an easily navigable pedestrian trail. A complete walking circumnavigation is less than 6 kilometers, with only a little up and down. There is not much public access to the water itself, but at the end of the pavement there is a small beach with no services where swimming is possible. In June, there is a local strawberry festival centered in the town of Nemi that attracts many hikers. There is a museum for Caligula's ships, which were destroyed during WWII, on the north side of the lake, adjacent to the only restaurant near the shore. Both Nemi and Genzano have restaurants with great views of the water from above.

Why go? The lake provides for a nice walk on a pleasant day.

 Where? Nemi Lake is 27 kilometers southeast of central Rome. The easiest and best way to get there is by car, and it takes about an hour from Rome. The train into the *Castelli Romani* ends before it gets to Genzano di Roma in Albano Laziale, necessitating a taxi/bus from there.

 Cost and time? The walk around the lake takes about an hour. The hike up to the village of Nemi from the museum takes about 30 minutes. Walking is FREE.

Kids? The trail will be a challenge for strollers, but this is a nice walk. About half is on a dead-end road so you will still need to be mindful of cars.

 Guide? No need for a guide for exploring the lake or the villages, though the ship museum would be more interesting with one.

When? The walk around the lake will be enjoyable anytime out of the regular seasonal extremes: the heat of the day in summer, the rain, the coldest of winter.

FUN FACTS

✳ A 1,600-meter tunnel, or emissary, was built by ancient local people (the Latins) in the 4th or 5th century BC to lower the level of Lake Nemi and increase the available arable land in the crater. It also kept the Temple of Diana from being flooded and provided irrigation to farmers' fields outside and west of the crater.

✳ The tunnel was further exploited by Mussolini's engineers to drain the lake in order to excavate Caligula's ships. The intake can still be found on the west side of the lake.

✳ Rumors are that there could be a third ship still on the lake bottom.

Enrichment: Some of the finest archeological finds from Lago di Nemi *can now be found in the museum at* Palazzo Massimo *in Rome. On the way to the lake from Rome you will pass through Castel Gandolfo, where many recent popes have spent their summers, and Ariccia, which is famous for* porchetta. *An excellent way to finish off a day hiking around the lake would be eating* porchetta *in a* fraschetta *in Ariccia.*

www.polomusealelazio.beniculturali.it/index.php?it/229/
museo-nazionale-delle-navi-romane

The Rivers

River Rafting

There are at least three commercial river rafting companies within an easy day trip from Rome. Roma Rafting runs half-day trips on the Tiber River through the heart of Rome. This is more of an opportunity to learn about the history of Rome from the river's point of view, though there are a couple of rapids to increase your heart rate toward the end of the trip. Vivere l'Aniene is based in the town of Subiaco and runs trips on the Aniene River, and Rafting Marmore is based in Papigno, Umbria, and runs trips on the Nera River. Both the Aniene and Nera are tributaries of the Tiber.

The Aniene at Subiaco is a relatively narrow river, chilly and refreshing, with several thrilling "drops" along the way. The Nera is fed by the Velino River, which feeds *Cascate delle Marmore* (Marmore Falls), the ancient man-made waterfall that is turned on and off on a schedule. This means that rafting also follows this schedule because there isn't as much water when the falls are off. At those times, Rafting Marmore guides low-water river trekking.

Why go? For these companies, there are really two different reasons to go rafting: in Roma Rafting's case, you get a guided river ride to learn more about the history of Rome and see the city from the river up; for the other two companies, you get a thrill ride through river rapids on an inflatable boat captained by professional river guides.

 Where? The put-in for the trip on the Tiber with Roma Rafting is at *Ponte Milvio*, which is about 5 kilometers north of *Piazza Venezia*. The take-out is at *Ponte Palatino* on the south side of Tiber Island, which is less than a kilometer from *Piazza Venezia*. Public transit can get you to and from both places. Vivere l'Aniene in Subiaco is about 50 kilometers east of central Rome and it takes about an hour to drive there. A bus can also get you there from Tiburtina

Rafting Marmore

Station in Rome in about 90 minutes, starting at about €4/person. Rafting Marmore in Papigno is 75 kilometers north of Rome. It takes about 90 minutes to drive there. It's also possible to get there through a combination of trains and buses.

 Cost and time? All of the rafting trips are generally half-day affairs. Prices vary by company: Roma Rafting trips start at €45/person, while Vivere l'Aniene and Rafting Marmore start at €50/person.

 Kids? Vivere l'Aniene will take kids as young as two years old. Rafting Marmore has an age limit of 18 for its regular rafting, but also has less strenuous "soft" rafting for kids as young as four. Oddly, Rafting Marmore also has a maximum age of 55 to 60, depending on the intensity of the trip, and they have a weight limit of 100 kilograms.

 Guide? All of these rafting trips are led by professional river guides, but they are often knowledgeable about the surrounding area as well.

 When? River rafting is most often a summer pursuit as most people get soaked going through the rapids, though the Tiber River trips tend to be less wet. Roma Rafting suggests the best rafting season is April to October.

FUN FACTS

* River rafting is an American invention, born on the wild rivers of the western US in the early 19th century.
* The difficulty of rivers is rated on a scale of one to six, with one being moving flat water and six being unnavigable. Commercial rafting trips take place on class I through V rivers.

Enrichment: Both Roma Rafting and Vivere l'Aniene also do trips at night, which can include an aperitivo. Roma Rafting runs other river trips around Rome, including the lower Aniene (just ask them). Vivere l'Aniene and Rafting Marmore lead many other thrilling river adventures, like canyoning and kayaking. Rafting Marmore also has a thing called Hydrospeed, which is something like downriver boogie boarding. Vivere l'Aniene even combines a rafting trip with beer tasting!

www.romarafting.com/en
www.viverelaniene.com
www.raftingmarmore.com/en

Canyoning

Canyoning, or canyoneering in America, is basically scrambling up and down stream courses that have created rocky gorges on the landscape. It combines a variety of techniques from wading through creeks to climbing, swimming, and rappelling. The equipment used includes wetsuits (with booties and hood), life jackets, helmets, climbing harnesses, climbing rope, and climbing/rappelling hardware.

There are at least two canyoning companies running commercial trips in Lazio. Vivere l'Aniene runs trips through the canyon of the Aniene River that include the waterfall above *Laghetto di San Benedetto*. Madmad Canyoning runs trips on at least four creeks that each have their own character.

Why go? Canyoning appeals to many of our childhood exploration instincts: playing in a creek, climbing on rocks, and scouting out what's around that next corner. Think of it as river trekking combined with rappelling down a waterfall — and it's a great way to cool off in the summer. Some of the trips will require the ability to swim while others do not, but all of them require you to get wet. It's an adventurous family bonding experience!

Where? Canyoning occurs in many gorges throughout Lazio. Getting to the gorges will generally require a car since they are usually located away from public transportation. While Madmad operates from the many locations where they arrange to meet their clients, Vivere l'Aniene is based out of their building in the town of Subiaco, 50 kilometers east of Rome.

Cost and time? The cost and length of each canyoning trip depends on the individual gorge. They typically start at about €40/

person, which includes the guide and equipment rental. Trips usually last two to four hours.

 Kids? The canyoning companies have minimum ages for their trips based on the physical difficulty of the individual gorge, ranging from 11 to 16 years of age.

 Guide? Canyoning is an adventure sport, so as a beginner, you really shouldn't go without a professional guide who stresses safety as their first concern.

Madman Canyoning

When? The best time to go canyoning depends on the specific environmental conditions of each canyon, namely the level of the water flow. Check with the guiding company for the optimal season for the best experience.

FUN FACTS

* The "father" of modern caving and canyoning is Frenchman E.O. Martel, who abandoned his law practice in the late 1800s to explore caves and gorges from Slovenia to Ireland to the United States. He explored over 1,500 caves and wrote 780 articles and 20 books on the subject.
* Canyoning is called "kloofing" in South Africa.
* The dangers of canyoning include hypothermia, flash floods, and rock fall. Additional safety equipment for canyoning includes a headlamp, a whistle, and a waterproof dry bag.
* In Lazio, even in the summer, the stream water is almost always cold.

Enrichment: Less technical canyoning is also possible (i.e., without a commercial outfitter), like wading the Cremera River into the Etruscan tunnel (Ponte Sodo) in Parco di Veio, or Le Gole del Farfa near the Farfa Abbey. Canyoning uses some of the same skills and tools as caving and river rafting, which are also adventures in this book.

  www.canyoning-italy.com
  www.viverelaniene.com/activity/canyoning-subiaco-rome

The Pools

Terme di Viterbo

Hot springs form where groundwater, heated by radioactive decay at the earth's core, emerges from the earth's surface. Outside the city of Viterbo, volcanic heat and subsurface water have combined to create a plethora of hot springs along a 12-kilometer fault line. The springs have a relatively high mineral content, namely sulfur, calcium, and magnesium, and have been popular for millennia for their therapeutic benefits.

The hot springs of Viterbo vary widely, from the small "wild" pools with few frills that are most frequented by locals, to the big spa complexes with hotels and restaurants that bring bathers on buses all the way from Rome. The smaller places include *Terme delle Masse di San Sisto*, *Terme del Bagnaccio*, *Piscine Carletti*, and *Terme del Bullicame*. The biggest and most famous spa is the *Terme dei Papi*, so named because popes have been coming to Viterbo for the "cure" for centuries.

Why go? Whether you need the curative powers of the mineral hot springs or are just after a cultural hot tub experience, Viterbo has what you're looking for, from rustic natural pools to elegant spa treatments. Each of the hot springs typically has several pools of varying temperatures so you can find one that is comfortable. The smaller places tend to be run by local community associations and may have a garden or a kiosk selling refreshments. The larger spas will have more services, like changing rooms, showers, and additional kinds of spa treatments. But the water is basically the same, so choose whichever suits you best.

 Where? Viterbo is 66 kilometers north-northwest of Rome and it takes about an hour and a half to drive there. Frequent trains from Rome-Termini to Viterbo take slightly longer. A roundtrip bus leaves *Piazza del Popolo* every morning at 9 am for *Terme dei Papi* and returns at 4 for only €8/person.

 Cost and time? The small hot springs are either FREE or require a modest "membership" fee to contribute to the maintenance of the pools. If you plan to visit regularly, they may even have an annual pass. The posher hotels can be quite expensive for elaborate spa treatments, but weekday admission to the pool at *Terme dei Papi* is only €12/person.

 Kids? Kids are welcome at the hot springs but the atmosphere is not about playing, it's about soaking. Though some pools can be festive, most are more serious. *Terme dei Papi* limits kids to their big outdoor pool.

 Guide? No, but there is an established etiquette for visiting a hot springs: proper attire (robe and flip-flops), how/where to change clothes, which pool to go into first. Expect to feel a little lost the first time you go, but you'll know what you're doing on successive visits.

 When? Fall, winter, and spring are the best time to go to the hot springs because the summer is too warm to want to get into the water. Even the rain doesn't have to be a deterrent, except when changing clothes. *Terme dei Papi* is open late on Saturday nights (from 9 pm to 1 am) and closed on Tuesdays for cleaning.

FUN FACTS

* Many people come to the hot springs as prescribed by their doctor for therapeutic treatment for various skin, cardiac, circulatory, or respiratory issues.
* In the early 14th century, Dante helped immortalize the hot springs of Viterbo by writing in Canto XVI of his epic poem *Inferno*, "As from the Bullicame a streamlet which the sinful women share amongst themselves; so this ran down across the sand."

Enrichment: As hot springs tend to zap your energy even though you're only soaking in a pool, driving back to Rome afterward can be difficult. Since there are many interesting things to do in and around Viterbo, it's easy to make a trip to the hot springs into a weekend excursion. Other sights nearby include the Palace of the Popes, Tuscania, Villa Lante, *and* Sacro Bosco *in Bomarzo.*

www.termediviterbo.it
www.termedeipapi.it
www.thermaoasi.com

QC Terme Roma

QC Terme Roma is a commercial wellness spa, 5-star hotel, and restaurant in Fiumicino, not far from the airport. Though all three can be visited independently, together they provide a particularly elegant experience. The spa is the primary attraction however, offering a quick and luxurious escape from hectic city life. It provides a multitude of spa treatments that include hot and cold pools, hydro massage, steam bath, sauna, massage, and "emotional" showers. The beautiful villa and garden setting have the perfect cultivated atmosphere for an adventure in relaxation.

Why go? Admittedly, *QC Terme Roma* is not cheap, but you owe it to yourself to get pampered once in a while, and the quiet comfort factor here is as high as it gets. In addition to the spa activities already mentioned, there is also a treatment lunch (for an extra cost), and later in the afternoon there is an "aperiterme" (included), the spa's version of an *aperitivo*. There are many options for quiet contemplation in a myriad of comfortable niches and nooks. To complete your escape from urban hassles, leave your cell phone in the car.

 Where? *QC Terme Roma* is 22 kilometers southwest of *Piazza Venezia*, adjacent to the airport in Fiumicino. It takes about half an hour to drive there from central Rome. It is also possible to take a short taxi ride from the airport after taking the Leonardo Express train from Rome-Termini station.

 Cost and time? Admission to the spa starts at €42/person, and there is a matrix of costs depending on the time of day that you arrive and the treatments that you desire. The entrance fee includes a white robe, towel, and slippers. Check their website for details. A room for the night starts at about €180.

Kids? Children under 14 are not allowed in the spa.

Guide? No.

When? The cheapest admission is after 7:30 pm, and the spa is open until 11 pm. If you have an early flight out of Rome in the morning, why not spend your last evening at the spa and hotel?

FUN FACTS

* Unlike the mineral hot springs found near Viterbo, the water at this spa does not have special medicinal qualities.
* There are many wellness spas of various kinds throughout Rome, some associated with hotels.

Enrichment: *This adventure will certainly be enriched by a bottle of prosecco. QC Terme Roma is very close to the ancient archeological sites of Portus and Ostia Antica.*

≡ www.qcterme.com/en/roma

The Agriturismo

An *agriturismo* can be many things, but basically it is an independently owned farmstay. Beyond that, it could be anything from a rustic restaurant in the country to a plush resort-style experience with food, lodging, and a swimming pool. What they have in common is a getaway opportunity for anyone that wants to support private rural farmers as entrepreneurs.

Why go? First of all, the food at *agriturismi* is often fantastic, using fresh local produce and family recipes. Generally, you'd be hard-pressed to tell the difference between an *agriturismo* and an excellent "regular" restaurant. Sometimes an *agriturismo* restaurant will have a menu to choose from, other times it will have a set menu of the food they have available. This tends to change by the season. Secondly, it offers a great opportunity to escape from the city and discover the Italian countryside up-close. There is often the chance to stroll in an olive grove or vineyard, meet the cows or the sheep, or hang out by the pool. And thirdly, the lodging can run the gamut from white sheets and chocolates to self-contained apartments, so you can choose the place that best suits what you're looking for.

 Where? There are hundreds of *agriturismi* all over the Italian landscape. Since they are, by definition, in rural areas, public

Agriturismo La Licina Spoleto

transportation is not the easiest way to get to them. You will most likely need a car. Of course, there is an excellent website that helps you find the most appropriate farmstay for you. Prior reservations are important so that they can prepare for your arrival.

 Cost and time? You can stay for only a meal, overnight, or for the week, so the time and cost depend on you. But the value is usually quite high!

 Kids? Yes! Every *agriturismo* is different of course, but kids generally enjoy visiting farms and many of the *agriturismi* cater specifically to families.

 Guide? Not needed.

 When? Anytime you want to get out of the city. The *agriturismi* that are adjacent to lakes or have a swimming pool are particularly attractive on hot summer weekends.

FUN FACTS

* *Agriturismi* are certified by regional governments throughout Italy to maintain standards.
* Staying at an *agriturismo* is not only a fun cultural experience, it also helps to maintain the lifestyle of small Italian family farms. There are approximately 17,000 *agriturismi* in Italy.

Enrichment: *When you are outside of Rome on other adventures and decide at the 11th hour that maybe you would rather stay the night instead of driving back to the city, try searching "agriturismo" on the mapping app on your phone. It will highlight the nearest farmstays and local restaurants and may give you some fantastic options.*

≡ www.agriturismo.it/en

Epilogue

The world has changed a lot in the time it has taken to write about the adventures in this book. When the COVID-19 pandemic swept across the world, international travel was halted, museums and archeological sites were closed, and much of the joy of discovering our planet was put into hibernation. But as a result, we learned that staying closer to home could actually be healthier and more sustainable than ticking off distant destinations. As our world gradually reopens, we believe these lessons learned will continue to enlighten our travel choices and underscore the great value of slower, more intentional adventures.

We hope you find this book useful in deepening your appreciation of a truly amazing and unique city. But it is about more than just the fantastic city of Rome: it is about cherishing lifelong learning and the diversity of educational opportunities for us and our kids. And it is about finding adventures and beauty in the details of everyday life and acknowledging the wonders of all the people on this planet — past, present, and future.

Good luck, be safe, stay healthy, and have fun!

List of Adventures for a Rainy Day

V Villa Giulia

X Catacombs of Rome

XVII Crypta Balbi

XXIX Palazzo Farnese of Rome

XXXII Palazzo Altemps

XLV Soratte Bunker in Sant'Oreste

XLVIII Doria Pamphilj Gallery

XLIX Palazzo Barberini

XLX Palazzo Corsini

LI Roman Churches

LII Villa Farnesina

LIII Palazzo Colonna

LIV Santo Stefano Rotondo

LVI National Gallery of Modern and Contemporary Art

LVII The MAXXI

LVIII Centrale Montemartini

LXXXV Caving

List of Adventures for Kids Under 10

VII Ostia Antica

IX The Aqueduct Park

XVI Villa of Tiberius at Sperlonga

XVIII Castel Sant'Angelo

XXVII Garden of Ninfa

XXX Villa Borghese

XXXV Villa d'Este in Tivoli

XXXVII Castello di Bracciano

XLI Villa Torlonia

XLII Villa Ada

LVIV Urban Murals

LXII Giardino dei Tarocchi

LXVIII to LXXII The Hill Towns

LXXIV SAID dal 1923

LXXXVI to XC The Sea Beaches

XCI to XCVIII The Lakes

CIII The Agriturismo

Maps

* Not bound to a single point, more information in respective adventure.

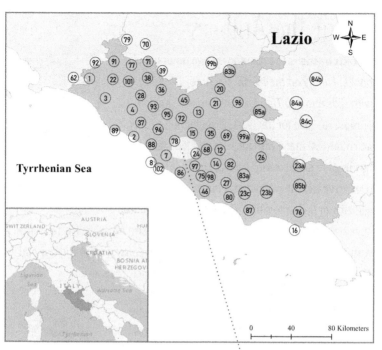

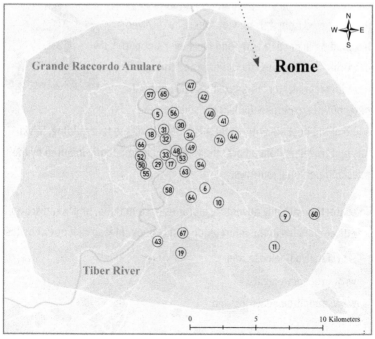

About the Authors

Bill Richards is the coauthor of two other travel books, *Family on the Loose: The Art of Traveling with Kids* and *100 Tips for Traveling with Kids in Europe*. His love for travel has brought him to over 40 countries, many with his wife and kids, and he has lived in six countries on four continents. For over 30 years, Bill worked as a forest ecologist specializing in the restoration of habitat for rare wildlife species primarily in the Pacific Northwest of North America. His technical writing has appeared in scientific journals like *Conservation Biology* and *Natural Areas Journal*. He has lived in Rome since 2018.

Silvia Prosperi is a licensed tour guide in Rome and Lazio. Born and raised in Rome, she has traveled extensively in Europe and beyond, but has never strayed from Italy for very long. She received her guiding license in 2009 and has never stopped exploring and learning about Rome and the surrounding region. Her "to-see list" is still endlessly long, but her expertise made it possible to select some of the best adventures for this book. Thanks to tour guiding, Silvia has met travelers from all over the world and is constantly inspired by their tales and personal journeys.

To contact us with any adventure inquiries or comments, or if you discover any discrepancies in the information in this book, please visit our websites:

- www.familyontheloose.com
- www.afriendinrome.it
- www.aroundromedaytrips.com

Made in the USA
Las Vegas, NV
28 May 2022

49455458R00174